Pets

THE ART OF LIVING SERIES
Series Editor: Mark Vernon

From Plato to Bertrand Russell philosophers have engaged wide audiences on matters of life and death. *The Art of Living* series aims to open up philosophy's riches to a wider public once again. Taking its lead from the concerns of the ancient Greek philosophers, the series asks the question "How should we live?". Authors draw on their own personal reflections to write philosophy that seeks to enrich, stimulate and challenge the reader's thoughts about their own life. In a world where people are searching for new insights and sources of meaning, *The Art of Living* series showcases the value of philosophy and reveals it as a great untapped resource for our age.

Published
Clothes   *John Harvey*
Deception   *Ziyad Marar*
Fame   *Mark Rowlands*
Hunger   *Raymond Tallis*
Illness   *Havi Carel*
Pets   *Erica Fudge*
Sport   *Colin McGinn*
Wellbeing   *Mark Vernon*
Work   *Lars Svendsen*

Forthcoming
Death   *Todd May*
Middle Age   *Chris Hamilton*
Sex   *Seiriol Morgan*

Pets

Erica Fudge

ACUMEN

For Julie and Macsen

First published in 2008 by Acumen

Acumen Publishing Limited
Stocksfield Hall
Stocksfield
NE43 7TN
www.acumenpublishing.co.uk

ISBN: 978-1-84465-156-6

British Library Cataloguing-in-Publication Data
A catalogue record for this book is available
from the British Library.

Designed and typeset by Kate Williams, Swansea.
Printed and bound by Biddles Ltd, King's Lynn.

Contents

Acknowledgements

As ever, when a book has one name attached to it that name usually hides all the help that has been received from numerous other people (although, sadly, the errors belong to one person alone). I have had a great deal of help throughout the process of writing this book. Teaching relief from Middlesex University has given me time. Mark Vernon and Steven Gerrard have taken the ideas through to their final stage with care and attention and Kate Williams edited the text helpfully and attentively. Tessa Fudge, Simon Glendinning and Donna Haraway offered comments and suggestions at an early stage that were extremely useful in helping me to put the final work together. Camaraderie and references have come from: Neil Badmington, Steve Baker, Sally Borrell, Carolyn Burdett, Jonathan Burt, Phil Cole, Diana Donald, Hilda Kean, Rachel Malik, Garry Marvin, Bob McKay, Laurent Milesi, Lawrence Normand, Clare Palmer, Stella Sandford, Julie Ann Smith and Sue Wiseman. Thanks go to all of them.

1. Introduction

Picture the scene: anthropologist and novelist Elizabeth Marshall Thomas, notebook and pencil in hand, trailing her friend's dog Misha through the streets of Cambridge, Massachusetts. Her aim: to find out what this dog does when it is outside the human home. Her starting-point: wonder. She writes:

> Here was a dog who never fell through the ice on the Charles River, a dog who never touched the poison baits set out by certain citizens for raccoons and other trash-marauders, a dog who was never mauled by other dogs. Misha always came back from his journeys feeling fine, ready for a light meal and a rest before going out again. How did he do it?   (2003: 2–3)

These "dogological studies", as she terms them, form the basis of her bestselling book *The Hidden Life of Dogs*, and offer, I think, an extreme version of the great fascination for pets shared by so many in Western culture today. Thomas's travelling through the city streets after a dog is asking a question that other pet owners have also asked themselves: how can we come to know this other being that is simultaneously in our home and utterly alien?

Here is not the place to retell Thomas's stories; as with many texts mentioned in what follows, you might want to read them for yourself if you haven't already. What is of particular interest to me is the fact that Thomas's study seems on the surface to rely on what she sees. And yet, without recognizing it explicitly, the answers to her questions about the dogs she lives with and studies actually come from two places: from her experience of watching them, and from her reading. She writes: "One by one, dog secrets were revealed through a series of adventures, some of them dangerous, all of them interesting. Misha was Odysseus, and Cambridge was the wine-dark sea" (*ibid*.: 17). The adventures she speaks of are empirical facts – they really are undertaken by her and Misha. But one of the explanatory frameworks Thomas uses to make sense of these adventures is imagined: the Greek myth of Odysseus.

Thomas's reliance on stories alongside experience – on Homer as well as her home life – to make sense of her dogs' worlds is something that will be repeated in what follows here. I turn frequently to the role of the imagination in thinking about pets for a number of reasons. First, imagination lets us construct ideal worlds and deal with the sometimes painful realities of everyday living. Thus, in the stories we tell and are told can be found some of the hopes and anxieties of our lives. Secondly, in the particular human–animal relationship discussed in this book, imagination permits us to anthropomorphize: to make pets into pseudo-humans. This is a transformation that allows for a conversation between the species, a conversation that is at the heart of the human–pet bond. Thirdly, imagination offers us the opportunity of thinking about other lives (both human and non-human) and exploring the possibility of other modes of perception. Such engagement with others, as we all know, is vital for living with other people as well as with other animals and is central to compassion and care for others, both human and animal, in that it is by imagining "that could be me" that fellow-feeling emerges. In these terms, I shall be arguing that thinking about pets relies on a form of imaginative thinking and, working in the other direction, imaginative thinking (and reading) can help us to contemplate pets.

But why think about pets in these terms now? There is, as we know, a pet industry out there, feeding human desires as well as animal ones. Millions of pounds are spent every year on pets: on food, healthcare, toys, clothing (a survey by the charity the Blue Cross suggested that in the UK in 2006 £5 billion was spent on pets, with an average of £231 per animal). In this context it is no surprise that there is also an abundance of reading material available for the interested pet lover; publishers only publish books they think will sell. So why write yet another one? What is it that this short book is doing that might be different from other studies of pets?

Many books focus on our relationships with pets from a personal perspective. Whether in memoirs, psychological studies or philosophical musings, writers use anecdotes to address the nature of the relationship and its meaning. There is, of course, a logical reason for this: pets live in our homes, they are crucial parts of our lives and are therefore significant in those terms. This book recognizes that fact, and acknowledges the importance of the personal mode in writing about pets, but itself does something rather different. It is not written from a personal perspective, and the reason for this choice is very simple: I think that it is time to assess what pets mean in a different way. The personal and anecdotal books that exist on pets have helped me to write what follows, certainly, but I think that it might be interesting, thought-provoking too, to contemplate our personal relationships with pets in more theoretical terms, and this is what I am doing here. What I hope will come out of such an interpretation is a different sense of the significance and meaning of pets in the modern Western world. Indeed, for the writers I look at in Chapter 4, for example, living with an animal forces a rethinking of some of the most important issues involved in what it means to live. By implication, without the animal the rethinking process might not have taken place and philosophy would have been cheated of some fascinating insights. Thus the ideas must be placed in a personal context, but the personal context can be read as just one part of the philosophical intervention that these animals have provoked.

It may seem to some readers that this distancing of the discussion of pets from the personal might work against the powerful emotional role that they play in the lives of the people they live with. My argument is that it actually allows us to revisit that emotional relationship in new terms. It allows us to find a way of recognizing both the affective and the philosophical importance of the animals that so many of us share our homes with. This assessment of pets in theoretical as well as emotional terms is part of a wider shift in thinking, and is related to a current movement that is taking place in scholarship in which writers and researchers are beginning to recognize that animals need to be thought about in more ways than they have been previously. There is an important underpinning to this shift: the way we imagine ourselves as humans changes over time (so a person living in the sixteenth century would have had a different conception of themselves to the one many of us have now), and right now, for a variety of reasons – the recognition of the environmental crisis that is upon us, the development of our understanding of our genetic closeness to animals, among others – non-humans are playing a central role in how we think about ourselves and our relation to the planet we live on. This re-imagining of ourselves is taking place in many areas of scholarship, beyond the disciplines of zoology, biology, ecology and so on, and is asking new questions about what a human, and what an animal, is. I shall take the nature of the writing of history as a way of explaining what I mean. What has happened in that discipline has also happened in others.

In the distant past most historians focused their attention on the activities of "great men" (with the occasional great woman, Elizabeth I, for example, thrown in for good measure). It was believed that it was by understanding the monarchs, diplomats and generals that the movements of the past could best be comprehended. This is perhaps true if your conception of the past focuses solely on diplomacy. To understand England's relationship with Spain during the reign of Elizabeth I, for example, a focus on court politics might be central. But if your understanding of the past recognizes that those much lower down the social scale than the monarchs and generals also had an important role to play then a study of Elizabeth's court might leave you wanting. This acknowledgement of the limitations of the history of "great men" led, in the mid-twentieth century, to the emergence of "history from below": a study of working-class life, movements and ideas that reflected the belief that history was also made there. But as this new field was becoming established other historians recognized further limitations even here, and women's history, histories of ethnicity and histories of sexuality were born. As such, the academic discipline of history – the writing of the past – mirrored the social developments of its time, and thus, for example, as the women's movement was agitating for equal rights in wider society in the late 1960s and 1970s so women's history was being written at that time by feminist historians. This new history highlighted the roles that women had played in the past and showed how limited and sexist previous conceptions of the past had been. The new history was one more strand of the women's movement.

More recently another new focus has emerged in the writing of history: the history of animals. Many scholars in this new field argue that it is impossible to understand human history without also understanding the role that animals played in that history because animals have always held key positions in so-called human society. For this reason the focus of historical writing has shifted, if you like, from looking at the farmer in isolation to contemplating the cows and the farmer. But for historians involved in this field, writing the history of animals is not simply including animals in the historian's purview because they are there; it is doing two other things. First, it is writing a more complete history of humanity: imagine a history of the home without at least a chapter on pets, for example (such histories exist), and you might get my point. Secondly, including animals is also, and at the same time, recognizing a change in *opposition* of human and animal. Many modern philosophers like Derrida recognize that human–animal is not an opposition at all but actually a form of inter-reliance in that the human needs the animal to be human. Indeed, the American thinker Cary Wolfe has stated that "the animal has always been especially, frightfully nearby, always lying in wait at the very heart of the constitutive disavowals and self-constructing narratives enacted by that fantasy figure called 'the human'" (Wolfe 2003: 6).

We disavow (exclude, silence) the animal in order to constitute (make) ourselves, and thus silence – the failure to include animals in discussions of the nature of the home, for example – should not be read as a marker of indifference, but rather as a necessary and productive exclusion. It is by "disavowing" animals that we construct ourselves. And Wolfe's idea that the human is a "fantasy figure" opens up the possibility that categories such as "human" and "animal" might actually be more like those fictional creations, centaurs and satyrs, than we expect: all are imagined in particular ways at particular moments for particular purposes. We live, an argument such as Wolfe's proposes, as if "human" was an unquestionable status, but what we actually mean by "human" goes way beyond biology. The "human", to follow Wolfe's terminology, is a creature of dreams and not just of genes.

So if the human requires the animal to think about itself, then it is clear that the human does not exist in isolation: to contemplate the being we call human is to conjure up many beings that are not human. In these terms, the dominion of the human is undone because what a human is is already reliant on and in hock to animals. To say, with Aristotle and all those thinkers who followed him, that man is a rational animal is, after Derrida and Wolfe, not simply to assert human superiority. Such assertions actually do something very different: they recognize humans' dependence on and construction of animals without actually really thinking about what such dependence and construction might mean. Once we do think about it, and do recognize the role of animals in such ideas, we might have to rethink who it is that we think we are.

But this book is about pets and not about animals in general, and in many ways this might seem counter-intuitive. Pets have been regarded by some thinkers as degraded animals: what might be perceived as truly animal qualities of wildness and self-sufficiency have been removed from – bred out of – the pet and replaced with tameness and dependency. It would seem perhaps more philosophically rigorous to contemplate the lioness hunting on the savannah or the pack of dingoes running in the Australian outback rather than the domestic cat or dog. But the pet's status as a creature that is somewhere between the wild animal and the human is exactly what makes it so interesting for many thinkers. A pet is what the anthropologist Edmund Leach called "an ambiguous (and taboo-loaded) intermediate category" between "man" and "not man (animal)" (Leach 1966: 45). Pets are animals in the human home; Leach calls them "man-animals". And in crossing over the boundaries between human and animal pets can play a particular, and particularly meaningful, part in philosophical contemplations that focus on what it means to be human, where the human ends and what is not human begins. Pets offer philosophers, if not food for their table then a great deal of food for thought.

This has been the case for centuries. Famously, for example, the late-sixteenth-century essayist Michel de Montaigne condensed his enquiry into the nature and limitations of human knowledge into a brief glance at his pet cat: "When I play with my cat", he asked, "who knows if I am not a pastime to her more than she is to me?" (2003: 401). Who, he pondered, is the passive party in this relationship, and who the active one? Such scepticism about human power and animal inferiority, and about the human capacity to make the world (what would it mean for human status if a human is simply a cat's plaything?) can be traced in much current thinking and thus it should come as no surprise that Derrida, writing 400 years later, also turns to think about his cat. It is by contemplating the most familiar of boundaries – that between human and animal – and how it is breached by his pet, that he is able to challenge most effectively many of the assumptions that underlie conventional thinking in which the human is still believed to hold absolute power over the world. The potency of pets may not be the kind of jungle potency of wild animals, but it is a philosophical potency that should not be underestimated. And, as literary critic Marc Shell has written, "If there were no such beings as pets, we would breed them, for ourselves, in the imagination" (1986: 142). It is not just that pets are interesting creatures; they have a greater power than this – we *need* pets to think with too. This is an idea that is present in all that follows.

Numerous modern writers are thus turning to the animals sitting next to them as they contemplate some of the most profound and profoundly important issues of our times: the impact of globalization; the nature of human knowledge; the limits of human power. Their work offers us insights not only into the role of the pet in contemporary culture, but also into questions about the nature of the home, the human and the animal, and this book will trace some of the ways in which some modern writers have written about pets and have used pets to think with (the two are not always the same thing). It will also attempt to show, as I have already hinted, that thinking about pets also opens up new ways of conceptualizing the world. But it is not just that philosophy offers us new ways of thinking about pets; the influence works in the opposite direction as well – pets also offer philosophers new ways of thinking. The pet, if you like, is not just the object of thought here, it is also the producer.

I shall also be arguing in what follows that it is often in imaginative writing that the most interesting and challenging contemplations of the human–pet relation are found. The reason for this is, I think, not only because many modern novelists are engaged in what might be termed meditation on the arts of living, but also because contemplating a pet requires an imaginative leap. "What is my dog thinking?" is a question, as I shall show in Chapter 3, that might only be answered by attempting to think with a dog: something impossible to achieve and yet necessary to attempt by anyone who lives with a dog. And it is here that fiction has a role. Stories might allow us, as readers and thinkers, to find a path between the impossible and the necessary. The imagination might offer a way of bridging the chasm that seems to separate humans from animals.

So, alongside Thomas's questions – what is it that dogs do and how do they do it? – we might add another, rather different but also important query: what is it that we see when we look at our pets? For the thinkers I shall be turning to in this book, what we see when we look at our pets can be very different: we can be led to think about how it is that we live with these other beings alongside us; what adjustments they, and we, have to make for successful cohabitation; we can begin to see another being, and thus think about what being other means. We might see also how that other being, the pet, helps us to make our world what it is: while we house-train them, you might say, they world-train us. Finally, it is possible that, when looking at pets we might discover something more about who it is that we think we are. A discussion of pet ownership begins with a glance at a dog, you might say, and ends with contemplation of the nature of the human.

This book begins in the home, and explores the ways in which pets are linked to the concept of domestic stability in many of the most pervasive and persuasive stories we tell ourselves about them in the West. I shall use the dog, the most storied of all pet animals, as a way of tracing the changing ways in which we conceptualize the space we live in. Across a century of wars, economic booms and busts and globalization, dog tales are told that help us not only to make sense of that world, but also to explore its strengths and failings. Dogs, I shall argue, offer writers a means of thinking about human stability.

Chapter 3 moves from using pets as a means of thinking about something other than the animal itself and turns to explore the question of the animal mind. How can we know what a pet is thinking? Can we ever write about the pet without forcing our own human perspective on to it? Philosophers and novelists have pondered this question in ways that lead to links between the imagination and thinking about pets. There is, I shall argue, a need for an imaginative engagement – a leap of faith, if you like – in the human–pet relation that connects reading fiction with what writer and dog-owner Marjorie Garber (1997) has called "dog love".

Chapter 4 turns to some recent philosophical writings by Derrida, Donna Haraway and Julie Ann Smith that emerge out of living with pets. No longer in the realm of fiction, these writers think about and with the animals they live with, and they ask us to do so in ways that could never have been imagined by earlier thinkers. In this Derrida, Haraway and Smith challenge some of the underpinnings of conventional Western thought and offer new ways of exploring the three concepts I am most interested in here: the home, the human and the animal. In their worlds, reading is not just an engagement with the written word; it is part of an engagement with the animal that helps them to construct their lives differently.

The conclusion, however, will sound a note of caution. It will address a limit and danger in the human–pet bond. If thinking about pets opens up so many possibilities for reconceptualizing our worlds, here I turn to contemplate one other reality of living with pets. The human–pet relation is a fascinating source of philosophical meditation, but it is also, of course, a real relation and the actual and possible divergences of the two will be the focus here.

The series in which this book appears is called "The Art of Living", and I hope that in this exploration of the ways in which living with pets is contemplated in the modern world we can investigate some of the intellectual arts – philosophies, literatures – by which and in which we think in the modern world, as well as the everyday arts of imagination and compassion by which we live. And it is perhaps worth noting that this book might be of interest not only to those who share their homes with non-humans, but also to those who do not live with animals but who like to contemplate the art of living, for, whether you live with a pet or not, thinking, I would argue, always takes place with an animal in mind.

2. Living with pets

Pets are good to think with. But, of course, pets are also, or so many of the households that include non-humans tell us, good to live with. The two – thinking and living – are never separate, and it is important to begin with an obvious question that brings both together: what function do thinkers imagine that pets serve in the modern world? Or, to put it more simply: why do they think that so many people choose to live with pets?

There are, inevitably, a number of possible responses to these questions, and I begin this chapter by outlining a few of the more mournful suggestions (the book becomes more positive as it progresses). One of the core issues that emerges from discussions of the human–pet relation in this chapter is the role that the animal plays in the conceptualization of the home. This is a conceptualization that is often taken for granted; home is so familiar to us that we frequently forget to think about its meaning and our expectations of it. But a stable sense of home is vital to many orthodox conceptions of human selfhood. For example, artist and novelist John Berger writes that in what he calls "traditional societies", "Without a home … one was not only shelterless, but also lost in non-being, in unreality. Without a home everything was fragmentation" (1999: 56). This is an idea that persists into modernity. Home is more than bricks and mortar: it is, or so the proverb has it, "where the heart is". If we think a little about this well-known phrase we can see that something crucial is at stake. If home is where the heart is, then, by implication, our journeys away from home – to work, for example

– are journeys we do not undertake as full beings: we leave something, a crucial something, of ourselves behind us. It is when we return, when we close the front door and step into the familiar and safe space called home, that we become truly ourselves again, or so the myth has it; and it is to the construction and revision of one particular version of this link between identity and home that this chapter will turn. Pets, I want to argue, have real functions and imagined ones, and both are vital to any assessment of why we live with them. Indeed, it is by tracing various ways of thinking about the concept of home that we can begin to understand these most fully. In particular we can begin to contemplate who it is that we think we are when we live with animals.

But while such a way of opening up a discussion of pets might seem sensible (let's begin in the dog-basket and work outwards) it is not something that is recognized by all thinkers. Thus, for example, even as Berger reminds us how significant the concept of home is to our sense of self he, like so many others, remains silent about the presence and role of pets in that home, and this silence, I think, is significant. Silence, the excluding of animals from discussions, does not mean that there is nothing to be said about animals. Rather, we might regard the silence itself as an object of analysis. Studies of the human home have been written, and I imagine will continue to be written, that do not acknowledge or explore the presence of animals. This might sound like poor scholarship – disregarding the evidence in order to construct an argument – but in fact this exclusion has been naturalized, has been made to feel like a sensible response, because it helps us to establish who it is that we imagine we are. Pets are often regarded as beneath scholarly notice to the extent that the sense of the sentimental nature of human–pet relations can make scholarship that includes pets itself seem sentimental (and, of course, sentimental does not mean the same as emotional here; it has far more negative connotations). Thus ignoring pets can, in fact, be perceived as *more* scholarly than actually writing about them. Either way, such philosophical silencing I regard as another way of asserting the presence of that fantasy figure called the human who stands alone: dominant, controlled and powerful. Such humanist claims might be found in silences more than in articulation (indeed, the silence implies that we all know this, that we all agree with this, that we don't need to discuss this). To begin to think about the animals we live with is, thus, to begin to undo a humanist construction of the human.

But where some philosophical writing has failed to acknowledge the role of pets numerous novelists have made explicit the links between the home, the stability of the status of the human, and the relationship with the pet, and in this chapter I shall explore one key myth about the pet that can be traced in a number of works of fiction from the past hundred years, and will offer suggestions as to the nature of the work that this myth does in modern society. I shall trace in the constant re-use and revision of the story of the return of the lost dog the changes that have taken place in the social fabric of modernity and in a sense of who it is that we think we are. If the urbanization and breakdown of the extended family that were the product of the Industrial Revolution of the late-eighteenth and early-nineteenth centuries impacted on human–animal relations – which they surely did – then it should come as no surprise to find that some of the consequences of late-twentieth- and early-twenty-first-century globalization have also affected how humans give meaning to their pets and themselves.

Before we can begin to think about the home, however, we need to contemplate the function of that being called the pet. Unlike most other animals, such as domestic cattle or wild creatures, pets are given individual names (sometimes human names), they are fed human-like (if not human) food, they are (like humans) not eaten, and they are offered increasingly sophisticated healthcare (organ transplantation for pets is an increasing trend). For many of us, pets are simply among those beings we live with: they are animals that are kin. The inherent paradox here – of a member of a different species also being perceived as a member of the family – is, in many ways, unimportant to those who live with animals. Of course the cat is a cat and not a human, a cat owner's argument might go, but that does not mean that that cat cannot play a vital role in the household. Pet ownership is premised on the notion that it is possible to extend one's capacity to love beyond the limits of species; that one can have a truly affectionate and meaningful relationship with a being that is not human. This is something I return to in Chapter 3.

Contemporary writers, however, offer us another way of contemplating the pet. Without necessarily undermining the possibility of pet ownership being affectionate and emotionally rewarding some current ways of thinking invite us to regard the pet as having other meanings. Indeed, I want to argue that a key way of thinking about personal identity in contemporary thought might be enriched by a closer interrogation of the place, meaning and role of pets. To make that case I want to trace some of the contradictions that seem to persist in the nature and function of the pet. I shall then think about how these discussions get played out in one of the most potent myths of modern pethood: the story of Lassie.

The function of the pet

In his influential book *Dominance and Affection: The Making of Pets* Yi-Fu Tuan argued that a particularly sentimentalized view of pets "was uniquely developed in western Europe [in the nineteenth century] and, later, in North America" (1984: 112). He proposed that the reason that this date was so significant in human–pet relations was because it was then that "humans needed an outlet for their gestures of affection [as] this was becoming more difficult to find in modern society as it began to segment and isolate people into their private spheres" (*ibid.*: 112). For Tuan modern pets are different from, say, the pets of the ancient world, because they are a product of industrialization and urbanization.

Tuan is not the only thinker to regard the human–pet relation as tied up with human loss in the modern world. Sociologist Adrian Franklin, like Tuan, regards pets as making up for a lack in human lives: "Perhaps because we have given up all hope of a cosy community life", he writes, "or because new factors have combined to make close relationships between adults more insecure, ephemeral or fugitive, a close relationship with pets is now seen as good for us and perfectly 'normal' and acceptable". He goes on:

> pets provide a somewhat nostalgic set of old-fashioned comforts. They make long-term bonds with their human companions; they rarely run off with others; they are almost always pleased to see "their" humans; their apparent love is unconditional (and therefore secured) and they give the strong impression that they need humans as much as humans need them.
> (1999: 85)

Pets provide, he writes, "ontological security". They allow one to know, "almost without thinking about it, that key areas in one's life are stable, predictable and taken for granted" (*ibid.*). In his interpretation, pets give secure meaning to humans in an insecure modern world; they allow humans to live as if with a self-assured identity.

But, let's return to Edmund Leach's reading of the pet that I mentioned in the Introduction. For Leach, the pet is a boundary breaker: it is what he calls a "man-animal". He makes this claim, on the one hand, for literal reasons: because pets have crossed over from outside to inside. They are with us in our homes, while all other animals – wild, game, domestic – live outside (the only other animals that get inside are uninvited and we label them "vermin"). On the other hand, Leach's term "man-animal" also works because pets are boundary breakers for less literal reasons. They, as I have mentioned, have individual names like humans, they live with us as members of our families, and so on. They are thus figuratively breaking down the distinction between inside and outside because they are like us and not like us simultaneously, a fact summarized beautifully in Leach's hyphenated term "man-animal".

Proposing the pet as a such a being would seem to make problematic a theory that links pets to a notion of ontological security because one form of security that we give ourselves in the world is, after all, in the firmness of the boundaries we erect: inside is not outside; human is not animal; self is not other. Clarity, clarity, clarity. Being a vegetarian, for example, can be interpreted in relation to questions of boundaries, and regarded from this perspective as being a more secure – a clearer – stance to take than being a meat eater. Vegetarians, after all, have erected an absolute boundary between the edible and the inedible. For them all beings with animate life – snails, fish, humans, cows – are not to be eaten. This is clear and straightforward. It is the meat eaters who live with boundary confusion. They must continually make careful and complex decisions about where the boundary between the edible and the inedible exists. Humans cannot be eaten under any circumstances, the argument goes, but sheep can. Dogs, while not human, cannot be eaten, not because they do not taste nice, but because they are categorized differently from sheep: they are pets. Rabbits, however, can be pets and meat (although it is unlikely in most cases that one animal exists in both categories simultaneously). And so it goes on, revealing that, while meat eating seems to make clear human difference from animals – humans can produce and kill animals for consumption as if they were merely objects – it in fact simultaneously undoes a comfortable sense of human superiority. A close look at the underpinnings of meat eating reveals how insecure the categories of difference it proposes are. What is and is not edible is not a natural opposition: if I can eat a sheep, what stops me from eating a dog, a cat, a chimpanzee, a human? Vegetarians, in comparison, seem to have an easy life.

Likewise, pet ownership has a complex role in marking out human security. If all animals were excluded from the home then the boundaries that the home symbolizes – between inside and outside, friend and stranger, private and public, and so on – would seem to be always firmly in place and security would appear to be assured. The existence of a group of animals that live inside the human home, then, might be read as a challenge to such boundaries, and the cat-flap becomes, if you like, a marker of insecurity and a symbol of the threat represented by a pet. If the door of the home is meant to be a boundary between outside and inside then placing a hole in that door that can be constantly penetrated reveals instead the lack of security that is created by the pet. The inside and the outside cannot be separated as there is a being within the home who is of both worlds (is a "man-animal") and so contaminates (for want of a better word) one with the other. Clarity is gone.

The anthropologist Mary Douglas is helpful here: home, she has written, is "space under control" (1991: 289); it can be anywhere – location is not essential to the "homeliness" of the home. What is important is the control, and part of that control must concern what is and is not within. An uncontrolled space, in these terms, is unhomely, is not home, and a pet therefore can, once again, be interpreted as a destructive rather than productive presence. And we can use Douglas further in thinking about pets here. Borrowing her description of dirt as "matter out of place" (2006: 44), we could say that pets are animals out of place, and that in that "out-of-placedness" they disturb the hygiene of the boundaries that give us certainty about who we are. And so, against Franklin's idea that the pet offers ontological security in an insecure world, we could argue that pets *by their very nature* challenge some of the key boundaries by and in which we live and thus they cannot provide ontological security, but instead undermine it.

But, if this is the case then why do so many households include animals? If pets are so disturbing, why do we continue to live with them? Perhaps we should not be trying to think in such simplistic binary terms about boundaries here. Perhaps a sense of ambiguity – of inter-reliance – is more productive. Maybe it is because of the fact that the pet breaches a boundary, not despite it, that pets are so important in the modern world. Perhaps breaching the boundary – standing in the place of a human while being an animal – is the pet's function. If, as Franklin argues, a pet can fulfil the role of the completely loving spouse at a moment when divorce rates are so high and so many people live alone, or if it can stand in for the kin-network from which one is separated because of the economic migration that is so common nowadays, is not this powerful evidence for the value of pets?

But this is very negative. The idea that a pet is a replacement for a human, that living with a pet is living as if with another person, has within it the possibility of presenting the human–pet relation as somehow false, as a pretence, and that is not how many pet owners experience their relationship with the animals they share their homes with. For many the pet is loved and is an animal, and the two are not contradictory. And indeed, we can go further: the pet is loved *because* it is an animal. So, with this in mind, we need to further explore Franklin's claim for the pet's role in guaranteeing ontological security even if we can see that a pet in itself seems to challenge the very structures of meaning that offer such security. "What is the function of a pet?" remains a central question.

One convincing answer to this question is simple: despite challenging boundaries pets are ultimately at the whim of humans, and training, however mild, reveals this. It is here, I think, that we can see that Franklin may be right to emphasize the work that a pet can do in creating a sense of stability for the human. Here is a being that can reflect back to us our fragility even as it allows us to express a sense of power and control. Pets can support a hierarchy that reassures us of our status in a world in which status can seem so fragile and changeable. And because the relationship with the pet is experienced as one of pleasure – mutual pleasure – we ignore the apparently negative possibilities.

This is Tuan's interpretation as well. He turns from his argument that pets make up for a lack in human lives to look at the power structure that underpins the human–pet relation and sees something that might disturb many pet owners: domestication, he writes, "means domination" (1984: 99). Indeed he proposes that

> affection is not the opposite of dominance; rather it is dominance's anodyne – it is dominance with a human face. Dominance may be cruel and exploitative, with no hint of affection in it. What it produces is the victim. On the other hand, dominance may be combined with affection, and what it produces is the pet. (*Ibid.*: 1–2)

Tuan traces links between the art of topiary and the training of animals: where one transforms the plant into an unnatural shape, he argues, the other transforms the animal into "a docile and friendly pet" (*ibid.*: 108). This training does not need to be physically cruel (although, of course, it may be); this is not the point Tuan is making. He is proposing that the existence of pets in and of itself is representative of the human dominance. Indeed, Elizabeth Marshall Thomas, despite having a completely different (that is, more positive) view of human–pet relations from Tuan, comes to a similar conclusion. She writes that she made "no attempt at house-breaking" Inookshook, one of the third-generation dogs in her household, but instead watched as "her elders taught her … everything she needed to know" (2003: 97): this is dog training without human intervention. But even in this environment, which seems free from human influence, Thomas notes that her dogs were not "free to act naturally"; simply cohabiting with a human had always and forever changed the nature of the animal. (Here is not the place to get into the debate about the relationship of domestication to canine identity: I refer you to Susan McHugh's book *Dog*, which offers a helpful discussion of this issue.) Human dominance is less visible in Thomas's household for sure (the human is absent from the training), but it remains the foundation for the pet's life.

But dominance isn't all; even while he argues that it is central to human–animal relations, Tuan recognizes that for many humans the relationship with the pet is one of love, it is just, he argues, that such experiences of love often "veil" the presence of human dominance. Removing the veil can have some shocking consequences; it can allow a glimpse of possibilities that the emphasis on love shields us from. For Marjorie Spiegel, for example, the relation between dog and owner is very similar to that between slave and owner. She writes that "All independent actions [by the dog] are ... discouraged, and the dog learns that she will win approval ... by suppressing her own desires and conforming to those of the omnipotent human who legally owns her" (1988: 37). In this reading of the human–pet relation the pet is a perfect replacement for the absent human because it does not require the kinds of commitment that another human might: as Spiegel notes, "If at any point the master grows tired of his slave, she can simply be turned over to 'the pound', which euphemistically means that she will be quietly and secretly killed" (*ibid.*). In this reading of pet ownership, human control is absolute.

Pets, these writers propose, thus reassure us that, whatever happens outside the home, at home we humans are the absolute masters and mistresses of our own domains. In the realm that is the human household, the well-trained pet plays the role of the obedient and adoring subject and the owner is monarch of all he or she surveys (and the poorly trained pet, of course, reveals the limits of some people's hold on such power). We get stable meaning – ontological security – from the hierarchical relationship with the

well-trained animal even as the pet would seem to create ontological insecurity by the mere fact of its existence. Indeed, it could
be argued that it is the very difficulty of pets that makes them so
powerful in our creation of meaning. It is because they are animals
in the home – because they are simultaneously outside and inside
– that they are so valuable both to live with and to think with. They
are a constant reminder of the fragility of our status and at the same
time they show us how our status might be and can be secured.
From this perspective, it is certainly possible to see how a slight
change to proverbial wisdom might make sense: home, in fact, is
where the pet is.

The myth of the pet

In his 1980 essay entitled "Why Look at Animals?", John Berger
– who ignored animals in his discussion of home – argued, like
Tuan after him, that the rise in the number of pets in the past two
centuries is a marker of modernity: that it "is part of a withdrawal
into the private small family unit, decorated or furnished with
mementoes from the outside world, which is such a distinguishing
feature of consumer societies" (1980: 12). But Berger does not have
much more to say about pets than this because in "Why Look at
Animals?" he is looking at what he regards as the disappearance
of animals in the modern world and does not regard pets as fully,
authentically animal. "The pet", he writes:

> is either sterilised or sexually isolated, extremely limited in its
> exercise, deprived of almost all other animal contact, and fed
> with artificial foods. This is the material process which lies
> behind the truism that pets come to resemble their masters
> or mistresses. They are creatures of their owner's way of life.
>
> (*Ibid.*)

Berger's belittling of the pet is worth pausing over as it asks us to consider again what a pet is. His argument that pets are somehow not fully animal (they are too humanized) implicitly proposes a category of the authentic animal (the lioness on the savannah, the dingo in the outback might be exemplars of this "authenticity"). This animal, Berger seems to be arguing, lives apart from humans, and has meaning in and of itself. Its identity is natural to it, and is not constructed or created through a relationship with humans. But such a claim – that wild animals are the only real animals, that domestic ones (cattle as well as pet cats) are somehow fraudulent because created by humans – not only problematically asserts a category of the authentic, it also demeans those beings that live alongside us humans. Indeed, Berger's concept of the animal exemplifies, I think, yet another way in which the humanist concept of human status can be maintained. Such an argument can be most clearly traced in Berger's statement that pets are "deprived of almost all other animal contact". This is clearly not true. Pets do have contact with one other animal in particular: the species *Homo sapiens* is central to all of their lives. By refusing to classify humans as animals Berger posits the notion of the human as separate from animals; he implicitly proposes the human as fully comprehendible in isolation. That is, Berger, like numerous other thinkers, proposes that we can think about humans without thinking about any other species, as if humans were the centre and meaning of their own worlds, and this in an essay in which he is bewailing such a perspective. Pets, for Berger, are not animals.

But we should not forget that Berger reflects back to us a figure with whom we are familiar. His notion of the pet reveals an idea of the human that brings together some of the core assumptions of some of the most influential of Western philosophies: it is Aristotle's human – rational, distinct from animals. It also takes up ideas from the philosophy of René Descartes in the seventeenth century, which presented the human as a thinking being ("I think therefore I am",

Descartes declared). Such a human does not require any particular context – historical, geographical, social – or any other creatures to exist; human identity is secured by the self's inherent capacity to think. Berger's notion of the human also comes out of the ideas of Tom Paine and Thomas Jefferson in the late-eighteenth century. Theirs is a human who has rights: to freedom of thought, freedom from violence, freedom to pursue happiness, and so on. The underlying belief here is that the human is special, different from animals; it is a creature that possesses reason, and is thus able to be responsible. For thinkers such as Paine and Jefferson, rights are "inalienable"; they are inseparable from the human. Thus a loss of rights would be a loss of self, and a loss of human status. Slaves, we should remember, were treated like animals because slave owners doubted their full humanity. Berger reiterates all of these ideas without acknowledging that he is doing so when he asserts that pets are inauthentic animals "deprived of almost all other animal contact". For Berger, pets are not important, not because they do not exist but because they are, in his opinion, not truly animals. This is one reason, I think, why his later discussion of the home does not include animals.

But more than forty years before Berger's "Why Look at Animals?" was written another writer had explored the significance of the pet in the construction of the home. This writer simultaneously presented and complicated the humanist concept of the human, as is logical in a representation that pays attention to the presence and importance of the pet and thus innately undoes the idea of human isolation. This text – not obviously a piece of philosophy – serves a philosophical purpose here because, I suggest, it presents in the form of fiction an argument that is central to how we think about who it is that we are when we are most ourselves: at home. Indeed, imaginative fiction should be understood not only as a medium in which humans are able to build fantasies of their security and status, but also as a means by which writers are able to engage with the pressing issues of their times in the most imaginative of ways.

This is how I want to understand literature here: it is a particular and telling assessment of the nature of the human. Thus, a 1938 short story, that became a novel in 1940, that was made into a film in 1943, Eric Knight's *Lassie Come-Home* encapsulates many of the ideas about home, pets and being human that are most significant in the modern age. Indeed, *Lassie Come-Home* is, I think, the most explicit rendition of a story that humans have been telling themselves since the emergence of modernity about who it is that they are, but it is also a story about how much this self-construction work shields a terrible insecurity. *Lassie Come-Home*, if you like, takes the debate about the nature of being human after industrialization out of the realm of the abstractions of philosophy and into a concrete narrative about a boy and his dog.

The story of the dog's return home that is the focus of *Lassie Come-Home* has a long history. Historian Kathleen Kete notes that in nineteenth-century France – a period that she identifies as one of increasing bourgeois dog ownership – stories of "the long trek homeward of a faithful pet, unguided and against all odds ... were commonplace events ... and the object then of much serious concern" (1994: 22). She cites as an example the apparently true story of the novelist Victor Hugo's poodle, Baron, who travelled from Moscow to Paris to find his master. Such stories were the stuff of fiction as well. In Albert Payson Terhune's story *Lad: A Dog* of 1919, Lad's journey is much shorter than Baron's but just as meaningful. He is accidentally left in New York when he falls out of his Master's car and is forced to travel alone the thirty miles to "The Place", the New Jersey farm on which he lives. But it is Knight's *Lassie Come-Home* that is the most famous version of this story in the modern era. Set in Greenall Bridge, a fictional Yorkshire village, after the closure of the pit, *Lassie Come-Home* tells the tale of the Carracloughs, a mining family, who are forced to sell their prize collie to the local aristocrat to pay the bills. The dog continually escapes from the duke's kennels returning always to meet the

Carracloughs' son, Joe, from school. Eventually Lassie is taken to the duke's estate in the north of Scotland to be separated from the boy and prepared for dog shows. However, she escapes again, and much of the novel follows her arduous thousand-mile journey across Scotland and the north of England, back to the school gates in Greenall Bridge.

This all sounds like great escapism (literally and figuratively), but *Lassie Come-Home* carries with it more significant meaning. The novel is, I suggest, an important interrogation of the role of the pet in the construction of the human home and thus of the human. This becomes most apparent at the moment when Joe's fantasy of the dog's return appears to have come true: when Lassie comes home. Lassie's return is accompanied by a realization that, even after her extraordinary journey, she must still be given back to her owner, the duke. This realization breaks Joe's heart, and his mother's attempt to deal with him is harsh but pragmatic: "Tha must learn never to want anything i'life so hard as tha wants Lassie. It doesn't do" ([1940] 1981: 216). The boy's response to this adult reality is not childish; it is, you might say, ethological – it speaks of the actions of the dog and not the human and thus appears to offer up a significant perspective on the nature of the bond between the human and the pet that his mother is unaware of. "Ye don't understand, Mother. Ye don't understand", Joe says. "It ain't me that wants her. It's her that wants us – so terrible bad. That's what made her come home all that way. She wants us" (*ibid.*). This assertion of canine desire transforms the relationship between the dog and the humans around her in that it ensures that we recognize the mutuality of, rather than the dominance inherent in, that relationship. The journey home is made, after all, by the dog and not by the human, and as such Lassie is, as Garber has noted, not only Argus, Odysseus's dog who dies wagging his tail at the sight of his finally returned and disguised master in *The Odyssey*; Lassie is also Odysseus himself – the mythical "quest hero ... crossing a fearful and unknown territory in search of home and love" (1997: 54). The dog is both the object and the subject of the story.

As well as this we should remember that the "Come-Home" in the novel's title is hyphenated: that is, the title is not an order but a name. Such quibbling over a hyphen might sound like scholarly pedantry, but the point is an important one. In the final chapter of the novel Joe says to the dog, "ye brought us luck. 'Cause ye're a come-homer. Ye're my Lassie Come-Home. Lassie Come-Home. That's thy name! Lassie Come-Home" ([1940] 1981: 231). It is as if, as well as invoking the Greek myth – putting the Homer in the "come-homer", you might say – we are also witnessing a modern version of Adam's naming of the beasts, where, in Genesis 2:19, the first man of the Christian narrative gave names to the animals that were not mere labels but reflected truly the essence of those animals. Thus in *Lassie Come-Home*, "Come-Home" is the dog's name and it is also a declaration of the dog's nature; coming home is what she must do.

The book proposes, then, two possibilities about the nature of the relationship between the human and the dog. On the one hand Knight suggests that it is the dog's desire to return to her master that is central ("it's her that wants us"), and on the other hand he offers the possibility that it is in the dog's nature (which, the novel tells us, is instinctive rather than reasonable) to return. Knight, in fact, has both of these potentially contradictory narratives working at once in *Lassie Come-Home*, and what emerges is the sense in which the relationship of the dog and the human is all the more natural and timeless because the return belongs with nature (the animal, instinct) and not with culture (the human, reason).

Thus *Lassie Come-Home* proposes an important way of under-standing the human–pet relationship that is a counterpoint to Tuan's argument that "Domestication means domination". The presence of the hyphen and all that it denotes in *Lassie Come-Home* challenges the idea that what underlies the bond between human and pet is the imperative "come home" in which the pet submits to human dominance. The hyphen, indeed, makes the pet's submission the pet's natural desire. Tuan states that the "harsh story behind the making of pets is forgotten" (1984: 108) under the veil of affection, and the mythical representation of the true and natural love of a dog for her boy found in *Lassie Come-Home* is, you might say, one of the most famous and powerful ways in which we perform this act of forgetting. From Tuan's perspective, such an image of the boy–dog relation places a veil between the reader and the domination that really lies at the heart of the human–pet relationship. The story makes a claim to the mutuality of the relation by emphasizing the "fact" that they want us perhaps even more than we want them.

Such a claim is not new to Knight; it had already been made in two novels that are key precursors to *Lassie Come-Home.* In Eleanor Atkinson's *Greyfriars Bobby*, Mr Traill, the kindly pub landlord, says "ilka dog aye chooses 'is ain maister" ([1912] 1994: 27). And likewise in *Lad: A Dog*, Terhune makes the distinction between "owner" and "Master" (he always writes this with a Godlike capital M) on a number of occasions and in a particular way: "Any man with money to make the purchase may become a dog's *owner*. But no man – spend he ever so much coin and food and tact in the effort – may become a dog's *Master* without the consent of the dog" ([1919] 1993: 13). But how is this consent to be represented? How can an animal that cannot engage in a written or verbal contract, agree to be a pet? For it is the animal's agreement that is so important if the relationship is to be understood as mutual. The expression of the dog's desire to be mastered – the communication of the animal's consent – is contained, of course, in the dog's arduous journey home. We let them go, but they just keep coming back.

These tales of returning dogs – of the lost pet found – continue to be told, and Jeffrey Moussaieff Masson offers an apparently simple interpretation of these events. He proposes that "What drives [these dogs] is love" (1997: 59). This answer to the issue of what it is that motivates these animals to travel such vast distances to find their masters seems inadequate, but perhaps this is simply because Masson's answer is so brief. Perhaps we need the meander – *The Incredible Journey*, as Sheila Burnford called her 1960 story of the return home of two dogs and a cat – to make the story about the pet's love palatable. And we do need, I think, the story to be palatable, because if we discount the existence of love we raise an important question: if dogs cannot love us why do we love them? Without the dog's desire such emotional responses as Odysseus's and Joe Carraclough's tears make no sense and the human–pet relation becomes simply what Tuan has identified as dominance veiled by affection.

The emphasis on Lassie's desire is thus, I think, the most resonant aspect of *Lassie Come-Home*. For, without such a perception of agreement by the pet, pet ownership becomes potentially meaningless, or at best merely an exercise in human control. In fact, the dog's consent to be mastered does more than give meaning to the relationship; it actually attests to the naturalness of pet ownership. But we can take this further. If it naturalizes the human–pet relation, then the dog's consent also makes natural the hierarchy inherent in that relation, and in making the hierarchy natural it cements the boundary between the human and the pet, as the love of the dog speaks for the natural mastery of the human. As such, pet ownership, as it is represented in *Lassie Come-Home* and those other novels, is what we might term a truly humanist pursuit in that it reiterates the natural and absolute difference between animal and human that persists in humanist thought. We might say, therefore, that if Descartes's *Meditations* is a central humanist text of the seventeenth century, and Paine's *Rights of Man* core to eighteenth-century humanism, so *Lassie Come-Home* is a key humanist myth of the twentieth century.

But that, of course, would be to ignore the fact that, as I have already argued, the pet can also be regarded as a creature that simultaneously breaches and solidifies boundaries. Humanist thought would have us believe that human status is natural and stable, and as I have argued *Lassie Come-Home* in many ways reiterates such humanism. However, we can also read Knight's novel as at the same time recognizing the powerful fantasy that is at work in such imaginings. It is the child – Joe Carraclough – who imagines stability coexisting with the presence of the dog:

> When they had had Lassie, [Joe thought,] the home had been comfortable and warm and fine and friendly. Now that she was gone nothing went right. So the answer was simple. If Lassie were only back again, then everything once more would be as it used to be.   ([1940] 1991: 63)

The adults, on the other hand, see something rather different. The dog is not a source of stability to them: it is a source of danger. Literally, Lassie costs too much; she undoes the family who love her. As Knight himself acknowledged in a letter written in 1940, *Lassie Come-Home* is "never so much [a story] of a dog, as it is of a man and a boy whose family is faced with what to them is a tremendous economic problem" (quoted in Wasserman 1993: 20). What happens when the novel is read with this sense of it in mind is that the concept of the stable human becomes nothing more than a childish fantasy, and the reality a very adult one. At the end of *Lassie Come-Home* the duke gives up his ownership of Lassie and offers Joe's father, Sam Carraclough the post of kennel-keeper on his estate. A deal is struck between the duke and Mrs Carraclough over his wages and the family's right to a cottage on that estate and the Carracloughs are thus saved from poverty and the humiliations of the dole, and the return of the dog does seem to be a return of the time when things were, as Joe had imagined, "comfortable and warm and fine and friendly". But this is still not the end. Eric Knight is a social(ist) realist, and the original short story on which the novel is based ends with a conversation between the duke and his granddaughter Priscilla about the deal Mrs Carraclough and the duke have just made – a version of which appears in the penultimate chapter of the novel.

> "And I thought you were supposed to be a hard man."
>
> "Fiddlesticks, m'dear. I'm a ruthless realist. For five years I've sworn I'd have that dog by hook or crook, and now, egad, at last I've got her."
>
> "Pooh! You had to buy the man before you could get his dog."
>
> "Well, perhaps that's not the worst part of the bargain."
>
> ([1938] 1990: 48)

Beneath the surface of the fairy-story element of *Lassie Come-Home* that focuses on the dog and her boy lies an uneasy (and very adult) truth: that employment has made Sam Carraclough, like a dog, simply a commodity in the possession of the local landowner; that there is an uncomfortable connection between the collier and the collie. *Lassie Come-Home*, thus, does represent the human of humanism but also reveals that, in a system in which humans can become objects, that vision of the human as free to choose, independent and coherent is nothing more than a child's fantasy.

And we can generalize from *Lassie Come-Home*: the pet, as Franklin proposed, provides humans with much-needed "ontological security". But it also reveals how far human ontological security – so readily apparent in humanist thought – needs animals to exist. And if humanism needs animals to exist then in that need it reveals that humans are not so separate from animals after all, and the importance of pets for thinking about human identity in modernity becomes clear. It is through thinking about the function of pets that we might get a clearer sense of who this being called the human is in the industrialized West.

But this story does not end there. The contemplation of what it means to be human in stories about dogs and homes continues to be a focus for contemporary writers. If *Lassie Come-Home* reflects the concerns of the economic depression of the 1920s and 1930s, more recent writers continue to invoke the myth of the dog coming home in order to reassess what it means to be human in an age of globalization. Once again, to the question "What is the function of a pet?" the answer comes back: it is one way in which we construct our humanity – or at least try to. In more recent renditions, however, this dog tale never comes to its mythical conclusion; the dog no longer comes home, and this failure tells us, I think, something about contemporary conceptions of humanity.

The loss of the pet

There are stories we want to hear and there are stories we want to ignore and the tale of the lost dog is in the latter category (the melancholy of those missing pet posters tacked to trees and taped to lampposts reminds us of how little we want to imagine such loss). Thus for the philosopher H. Peter Steeves the "agony" of the lost dog casts a shadow over the wonder of the dogs who return, and he once again invokes the story of Odysseus when he writes that the argument for the mutual nature of the human–dog relation is inseparable from the possibility of the story's failure. "Hearing only those stories in which he succeeds, we imagine any animal capable of the feat. The majority, of course, leave Penelope forever waiting" (2005: 31). Suddenly Lassie's journey seems very clearly to be the stuff of fiction, and the story of the come-home is also its other: the story of the forever-lost. Our fantasy is undone.

But this does not mean that the Lassie myth is fading in contemporary ideas: far from it. The Lassie myth is alive and well in contemporary thought, it is just that, as Steeves shows, it gets played out rather differently. As with *Lassie Come-Home* before them, contemporary novelists also draw links between humans and animals. If Sam Carraclough is owned just as Lassie is owned, so Paul Auster and John Berger (who had ignored pets in his non-fictional writings about home and demeaned them in his essay "Why Look at Animals?") have both written dog novels in which humans are, like dogs, lost. We can see in Auster's *Timbuktu* and Berger's *King: A Street Story*, both published in 1999, contemporary rehearsals of the modern myth. But for these authors, and other contemporary writers, the dog never gets home.

Berger's *King: A Street Story* is narrated by King, the dog of a homeless couple who are living in a makeshift community on waste ground outside a French city. Just as Franklin argued that pets provide humans with ontological security, so Berger has noted in his non-fiction, as we have seen, that home is a site of stability not only in geographical terms but in ontological ones too. Pets and homes fulfil the same function for the human; we construct ourselves in and from them. In Berger's novel, however, he shows us the opposite of such stability. In *King* the characters' lack of a home creates other instabilities in the text, including a key question as to whether the dog really is a dog after all, and whether we could actually tell the difference between a human and a dog if humans are homeless. The horror that lurks at the heart of this story is twofold. It is that homelessness is not simply a question of being unhoused, but is also a question about identity. His claim is that we need to think about the idea of homelessness in broader terms.

For Berger, being homeless is becoming a norm in the modern world. He has argued in his non-fiction that "Emigration, forced or chosen, across national frontiers or from village to metropolis is the quintessential experience of our time" (1991: 55). To be on the move rather than fixed in space is the nature of the modern world, and as such emigration can end without an endpoint; it can result in a transient life, in the life of a transient. We may have an address and still be homeless. In this reading of homelessness it is clear that there is no home for a dog to return to, and so no dog can ever be a come-home dog. In *King*, then, the Lassie myth is present – there is a dog and a conception of home – but that myth becomes impossible; it becomes, you might say, a story without a stable in a world without stability.

Berger is not alone in his analysis of the inherent transience of our experience of the modern world. The concept of the nomadism of contemporary life is fast becoming a critical commonplace; indeed, the contemporary cultural commentator John Durham Peters has argued that "The nomad is explicitly a hero of postmodernist thinking. ... The point of the nomad, as of the philosopher, is to invent concepts that defy settled power" (Peters 1999: 33). For him, it is not simply that nomadism is a way of life; it has also been constructed as a way of thinking. Philosophy is now a destabilization of "settled" (that is, stable and stabled) power; it is a revolt against ideas of stasis. Philosopher Zigmunt Bauman seems to support Peters's argument when he proposes in his 1998 study that movement is the common state of humanity after globalization. But he is less than celebratory about the impact of this fact. He proposes that there are now "two types of experience" of the world. "Tourists", he writes, "become wanderers and put the bitter-sweet dreams of homesickness above the comforts of home – because they want to" (1998: 92). Vagabonds, on the other hand, "are the waste of the world which has dedicated itself to tourist services". They are, "one may say, involuntary tourists" (*ibid.*: 92–3). There are no animals in Bauman's analysis, but the notion of the involuntary tourist is perhaps most obviously translated into fiction in Anne Tyler's 1985 novel, *The Accidental Tourist*, in which much of the action centres on the mourning father's training of his dead son's unruly corgi, Edward. This man, who writes books for salesmen who travel but want to remain at home, is also trying to reconstruct a fractured home around a dog.

Bauman's notion of the "involuntary tourist" can also be found being played out among non-humans in Berger's human and canine homeless community, forced out of their provisional homes and back on to the road again at the novel's end, and it is present once again in the second 1999 dog novel, Auster's *Timbuktu*. This begins with Willy G. Christmas, failed writer and dying, homeless son of Polish holocaust survivors, travelling with his faithful dog, Mr Bones, to find his former English teacher in Baltimore. Without a map, man and dog get lost and accidentally – involuntarily – find themselves at a local tourist attraction: 203 North Amity Street. It is, as the plaque on the wall reads, "Residence of Edgar Allan Poe, eighteen-thirty-two to eighteen-thirty-five. Open to the public April to December, Wednesday through Saturday, noon to three forty-five PM" (1999: 46). Even a home is a public space in this world of movement.

On the pavement outside Poe's house Willy collapses and is taken away in an ambulance, and the rest of the novel follows Mr Bones's adventures, which end with his suicide by running on to a six-lane highway. Dog suicides were a frequent part of stories of faithful pets in the nineteenth century, as Kete has shown, and Mr Bones's tale seems no different; his suicide is a kind of journey – this dog, like his mythical forbears, takes to the road in order to find his master. But Mr Bones will find his master not at the school gates in Yorkshire but in the imagined "next world", which Willy called Timbuktu. It is only in death, this novel proposes, that a true homecoming is possible. Here is no joy, no child's experience of stability.

These two end-of-millennium novels invoke, then, a conception of the human–dog relation that can be traced in *Lassie Come-Home* in that they recognize the link between human identity and the possession of a dog. However, these novels reflect an anxiety about the possibility of telling ourselves stories about human selfhood using the home and the dog as our markers. In an era of mass migration, social mobility, international travel and increasing home-lessness, to rely on a pet to explain away the horrors of the world no longer seems possible. For Knight, the dog could only really explain away horrors to the child; *Lassie Come-Home* ends, after all, with the adult acknowledgement of the links between the working man and the dog. But at least Knight could fantasize about the possibility of security. Contemporary novelists and philosophers, on the other hand, seem to engage much more fully with the failure of the stories we have told ourselves. Just as contemporary philosophy argues that humanism cannot contain its desire for the separate and supe-rior human, so these more recent novels reveal the impossibility of getting home in a world of constant movement. So indebted are we to the dog myth, however, that it is this that these novelists choose to use to show us that we are forever lost.

The cruellest version of the dog myth to appear in the past few years, and the one I will close this chapter with, is Dan Rhodes's 2003 novel *Timoleon Vieta Come Home*. This clearly invokes Knight's novel – a quotation from *Lassie Come-Home* is Rhodes' epigraph – but *Timoleon Vieta Come Home* also mocks our desire for Lassiean happy endings, and this is where its cruelty lies. Here the dog, Timoleon Vieta, is named after a book (the first and last words in the T–V volume of an encyclopedia), and is attempting to rejoin his master at his Umbrian villa after being abandoned in Rome. He has his throat cut just outside his master's gates. Here the "come home" lacks a hyphen: it is not a name, not part of the dog's character, but an order. And here, the novel ends with the dog's owner happily walking down the track from his house arm in arm with his lost lover, singing and laughing. He will, we know – although Rhodes leaves this to our imagination – soon find the body of Timoleon Vieta and his happiness will be destroyed. Once again, we want Lassie but instead we get a dead dog.

In the 2003 story the dog does answer the master's call, does try to come home, and yet the attempt will bring with it not joy but horror; not stability but chaos. Rhodes has us read *Timoleon Vieta Come Home* as if it was *Lassie Come-Home* and the cruelty is that we desperately want to do this. We want the dog to come home – we want the happy ending with its apparent stability, finality and completeness (a "drive towards completion" is what Kenneth Burke argued myth offers (quoted in Coupe 1997: 6). What we get instead is the realization that such stability, finality and completeness are the stuff of myth. In reality the dog does not get home; in reality the human is never made secure by the existence of a pet. But that does not mean, as these novels show, that we do not search for stability: that we will stop telling ourselves the story of Lassie.

The links between the presence of a dog in the home and the stability of human status continue to be made across the twentieth century and into the twenty-first, and it is perhaps this that we should consider to be one of the key functions of the pet in the modern era. If the early-twentieth-century dog myths were an attempt to rectify the objectification of the human under industrialization, the late-twentieth- and early-twenty-first-century dog myths tell of the impossibility of any such rectification, and yet the persistence of the Lassie myth in an age of globalization (another film version of the story appeared in 2005) reveals how much we still want the security that the pet apparently offers. The human home, it would seem, is never secure (whatever we might tell ourselves) and the presence of the pet – the "man-animal" that simultaneously constructs and undermines our identity in that home – merely marks our continuing dream of our own ontological security. It's just that now we fear that Lassie cannot come home. But that doesn't stop us dreaming that she will.

3. Thinking with pets

This is all very negative. So far the pet is interpreted as a being that makes up for an emptiness in modern life. It does not really figure as an animal in these analyses so much as a surrogate human. And the human owner in the relationships is not a pet lover but a being living in a world of make-believe in which an animal performs the role of the silent, utterly faithful human companion who is the absent but truly desired presence. In the texts referred to so far, then, thinkers have attempted to give meaning to the human–pet relation, but have only been able to do so by two means: first, by concentrating on the symbolic potential of the pet while ignoring the presence of the real animal; and secondly, by never really contemplating the positive possibilities of actually living with a pet. These two means are related, I think, and we need to try to find an alternative way of engaging with the presence of the animal that emphasizes its status *as animal* when we contemplate the meaning and role of the pet if we are to construct a more affirmative conception of human–pet relations. We can do this, I suggest, by looking not so much at what we think about living with animals as by contemplating what it is that we think pets actually are. This might sound paradoxical, looking at the lived relation by interrogating the thought one, but the two – living and thinking – are inseparable, and I hope I can show how living with a pet requires an understanding of it that must include a sense of its inner-being and not just its outer meaning.

So here is another question: not "What is the function of the pet in the life of a human?", but what might actually be more challenging:

what if loving an animal is not a fraudulent version of some other kind of loving? What if, as Marjorie Garber has proposed, "dog love is love", not simply a representation of, or a rehearsal for, love? What would such a kind of loving entail? It would mean, I suggest, that the pet would need to have a status that has not yet been traced. What that status is, and how it might be represented, is the focus of this chapter.

It is no coincidence, I think, that the assertion that "dog love is love" comes from a writer who is not only a dog lover but also a literary critic. Why no coincidence? Time and again we come across links between living with pets and writing and reading fiction. In the previous chapter I argued that novelists offer us some of the most insightful discussions of the meaning of the pet in modernity. This is one relation between the pet and the literary that I shall invoke again in this chapter. But I also want to go beyond this and see reading literature, as well as writing it, as a model of a mode of engagement that is particularly productive when thinking about pets.

Thus I shall, in this chapter, be tracing different ways of writing and reading (about) the nature of pets. The chapter is organized around three themes, all linked to the issue of imagination: knowledge, language and compassion. The first section questions whether we can ever know what goes on in the mind of an animal. Two responses, one negative and one positive, reveal the complexity of the problem and its centrality to ways of thinking about the status of pets. In the second section I look at constructions of human–pet communication and at the role of language in conceptions of human superiority. The final section turns to the question of compassion and argues that this should be interpreted in relation to questions of imaginative thinking, and that as such compassion can be felt for an animal. Finally, drawing an analogy between reading fiction and being compassionate I turn briefly to one dog novel that I think offers insight into all of the key issues of this chapter and allows us a glimpse into a way of thinking and living with pets that acknowledges and embraces some of the very real difficulties we face if we are to declare that dog love is love.

This chapter sits, then, as a counterpoint to the previous one. There I emphasized the constant use of the pet to symbolize something for humans: to represent a concept of home. What the dog itself thought or felt in all those stories was only important for what it told us about ourselves. This chapter looks beyond the silent, symbolic pet and finds something very different. It turns the tables on the previous chapter, if you like, and thinks not about giving pets meaning so much as recognizing that pets themselves can make meaning. I begin, however, at the other end of the debate, with a discussion about whether it is ever possible for a human to access the mind of an animal.

The being of a pet

What if all animal consciousness is inaccessible to humans? This is an assertion made by philosopher Thomas Nagel in his 1974 essay "What is it Like to be a Bat?" Here Nagel writes, "I assume we all believe that bats have experience … that there is something that it is like to be a bat" (1974: 438). Beginning from this perspective he notes that a bat uses sonar or echolocation to find its way around, and that "bat sonar, though clearly a form of perception, is not similar in its operation to any sense that we possess, and there is no reason to suppose that it is subjectively like anything we can experience or imagine". Nagel continues:

> It will not help to try to imagine that one has webbing on one's arms, which enables one to fly around at dusk and dawn catching small insects in one's mouth; that one has very poor vision, and perceives the surrounding world by a system of

> reflected high-frequency sound signals ... In so far as I can imagine this (which is not very far), it tells me only what it would be like for *me* to behave as a bat behaves. But that is not the question. I want to know what it is like for a *bat* to be a bat. (*Ibid.*: 439)

There is a crucial difference between a bat's experience of its own bat-ness and a human construction of bat-ness. The human construction, Nagel argues, will always be human and will therefore always transform the animal; it will always be anthropomorphic.

Nagel's assertion of the absolute impossibility of knowing what it is like to be a bat (and of course a bat here stands for all other animals) reveals the restrictions of the human mind when faced with non-humans. "Our own experience", he writes, "provides the basic material for our imagination, whose range is therefore limited" (ibid.). Indeed, he states not only that we can only ascribe experience to one who is "sufficiently similar" to ourselves because it is only then that we can "adopt his point of view", but also that "we will have as much difficulty understanding our own experience properly if we approach it from another point of view as we would if we tried to understand the experience of another species without taking up *its* point of view" (*ibid.*: 442). Nagel's reading is not, then, anthropocentric; it does not assume that human experience (the belief that there is something that it is like to be a human) is the only kind of experience possible. Just because we cannot know what it is like to be a bat, he argues, does not mean that we should assume that bats do not "have experiences fully comparable in richness of detail to our own" (*ibid.*: 440). Rather, Nagel recognizes that gaining access to the experience of any dissimilar being is almost always impossible because "I am restricted to the resources of my own mind, and those resources are inadequate to the task" (*ibid.*: 439) of imagining not only what it is like to be a bat but also what it is like to be anyone or anything far removed from myself.

Such a view of human–pet relations (if we restrict our reading of Nagel to that set of possibilities) would be utterly awful. It would mean not so much that the conversations we have with our animal friends are surrogate conversations for the ones we really want to have with our, by implication, *real* human friends: a perspective traced in the previous chapter. If Nagel is right, it might mean that any attempt to achieve anything more – to believe that dog love is love, for example – would be utterly pointless because there is no chance of any kind of cross-species comprehension emerging: no possibility of anything like mutual love existing in that relationship. If a cat is such an alien life form that I cannot imagine what it is like to be a cat, how can I possibly ascribe feelings or motivations to that cat without recognizing that those feelings and motivations are constructed by me and are therefore only partial representations – simply a reflection of the limitations of my own imagination? This is part of the philosophical anxiety, I think, that underpinned Montaigne's question: "When I play with my cat, who knows if I am not a pastime to her more than she is to me?" If I cannot comprehend what it is like to be a cat how can I ever expect to live happily with that cat?

J. M. Coetzee directly addresses Nagel's essay in his novella *The Lives of Animals*, which was published in the same year as *King* and *Timbuktu*, and in this response he reveals the dangers that lie both in Nagel's work and on the other side of the debate. Coetzee also allows us to see how thinking about animals may be tied up with thinking about reading and writing fiction: how the imagination has a role to play in both. An outline of the central ethical argument of the text shows how this works.

The Lives of Animals follows the fictional Australian novelist, Elizabeth Costello, as she gives two lectures on animals, ethics and literature at an American university. In the first lecture Costello outlines Nagel's argument and responds by offering a perspective that sits in absolute opposition to it. Nagel, Costello argues, is wrong when he proposes that "we need to be able to experience bat-life through the sense modalities of a bat". She continues:

> To be a living bat is to be full of being; being fully a bat is like being fully human, which is also to be full of being. Bat-being in the first case, human-being in the second, maybe; but those are secondary considerations. To be full of being is to live as a body-soul. One name for the experience of full being is *joy*.
>
> (1999b: 33)

For Costello, to shut down the possibility of contemplating the being of a bat is to silence the faculty of "*sympathy* ... that allows us to share at times the being of another". But this is not the only thing that sympathy does: "Sympathy", she states, "has everything to do with the subject and little to do with the object, the 'another', as we see at once when we think of the object not as a bat ... but as another human being". Costello does not only propose that the bat (and all the other animals that it stands in for) is a subject rather than an object; she goes one stage further and assumes that subject status is human status and that the bat should be regarded, therefore, "as another human being" (*ibid.*: 34).

The way Costello makes the case for the shared existence of bat and human – and it's never clear whether Coetzee agrees or disagrees with her point of view – is by turning to her capacity as a novelist. She emphasizes being in rather than experiencing the world, and claims omniscience from her position as an imaginer of other lives. Her fame as a novelist, Costello realizes, is based in part on her book *The House on Eccles Street*, which tells the story of Marion Bloom, wife of Leopold Bloom, the central character in James Joyce's *Ulysses*. Costello claims that her success in her novel provides evidence of what she believes the human imagination is capable of and in doing so she directly challenges Nagel's belief in its limitations. "Some years ago I wrote a book called *The House on Eccles Street*", she says:

> To write that book I had to think my way into the existence of Marion Bloom ... the point is *Marion Bloom never existed.* Marion Bloom was a figment of James Joyce's imagination. If I can think my way into the existence of a being who has never existed, then I can think my way into the existence of a bat or a chimpanzee or an oyster, any being with whom I share the substrate of life.　　　　　　　　　　　　　　　　(*Ibid.*: 35)

This is an argument that has far-reaching implications. Using the model of creative writing Costello is able to claim that she can "imagine" herself into the being of another, but her assumption that she can do this seems dangerously close to the idea of imagining what it would be like for a human to be a bat (rather than for a bat to be a bat) that Nagel regarded as evidence of the failure of the human imagination.

As well as this, if Nagel emphasizes human limitation, then Costello's model of sympathy in which the bat is figured "as another human being" reveals her theory of equality to be anthropomorphic in that it transforms the world into the human and is thus, paradoxically, anthropocentric. This is one of the logical traps of anthropomorphism. According to the German philosopher Martin Heidegger, what underlies the transformation of the world into the human is the belief, as Tom Tyler notes, quoting Heidegger, that "one knows 'ahead of time' what human beings are" (2003: 273). That is, for Heidegger, anthropomorphic thinking can only take place because there is always already in place a belief about what a human is, because one needs the human to be in place to be able to transform the world into one. As such anthropomorphism can be regarded as a product of humanist thought in that it regards the human as an unchanging and permanent feature of the world, and it sees humanity as the lens through which that world must be read. To imagine a bat "as another human being" is to assert the subject status of the non-human, but it is also to fail to imagine that there is any other way of being a subject in the world than being human.

This is the problem we face, then, when we attempt to live with animals. On the one hand – following Nagel – we can see that we cannot ever understand what it is like to be, say, a cat, and thus there must be an absence, a lack, at the heart of the relationship with the animal. On the other hand, we can claim – as Costello does – that we do have the capacity to comprehend animals because we have a capacity to imagine that reaches beyond what is different and traces out what is shared. This would seem helpful as a way of thinking about how we negotiate our relationships with pets. But, this position also implies that the human imagination has unlimited power in the world, and thus a humanist arrogance lurks dangerously nearby.

An unproblematic answer to Nagel is not to be found in Costello's argument, then. But, one of the strangest realizations that comes out of reading the real Nagel and the fictional Costello alongside each other is how they both appear to be one thing but end up being another. Arguing that we can never know what it is like to be a bat might seem to make the being of a bat unimportant: if we can never know, why should we try to figure it out? But in reality Nagel's argument does the opposite. His scepticism at this point does not undermine the status of animals; rather, it challenges humanist assumptions about the power of humans to construct and know the world. Following his thinking we can see that there are animals – many of them living in our homes – who share our world and who escape our understanding, and thus, from this perspective, living with a pet can be regarded as a powerful exercise in being humbled. Pet ownership, once again, can actually undo humanist thought. We look at our pets and, like Montaigne, realize that we do not, cannot, know everything.

Costello's assertion of the significance of all beings, on the other hand, would appear to be an egalitarian response in which human status is shared with the rest of the animal world. But this egalitarianism also reveals its opposite: it is not her sympathy for animals that differentiates Costello from Nagel (there is nothing to suggest that Nagel couldn't be, say, a vegan from his argument); it is her representation of the human that is so distinct from his. If Nagel's human is figured as lacking authority then Costello's human is full of power. She asserts that the human has the capacity to imagine every life, fictional and non-fictional, and is boundless in its ability to know. Her human is, in short, omniscient, God-like, rather like Lad's Master who was always spelled with a capital M. Ironically, it is the egalitarian argument that posits the superior human.

But this is not a paradox that is unique to Costello. Thinking about pets has always offered contradictory possibilities. According to James Serpell, it is inevitable that one anthropomorphizes when living with a pet. "Anthropomorphism", he writes:

> rules because any other interpretation of the animal's behavior – any suggestion that the pet might be motivated by other than human feelings and desires – instantly would devalue these relationships and place them on a more superficial and less rewarding footing. (2003: 91)

If it is inevitable that we turn our pets into humans, or at least human-like beings, in order to form close bonds with them it would seem that pet ownership is a challenge to human status. But (and we are back to questions of ontological security here) it could be argued that, in many ways, the boundaries that separate the human from the rest of the natural world are not actually challenged at all in the relationship with the pet: in the first place because the pet's animal-ness is blotted out and replaced with a construction of it as a pseudo-human; and in the second, because loving a pet does not automatically mean being an animal lover. As Marc Shell notes, "The institution of particular pethood depends upon the individual pet owner having a different relationship to his animal than he has to other animals" (1986: 126). Thus the boundaries of difference that might appear to be uprooted in the anthropomorphic relationship between the owner and the pet could actually still be in place; the home remains human because the pet is made human and all other non-human animals are excluded.

The anthropomorphism that sits at the heart of human–pet relations can also be taken to extremes that reiterate the emphasis on the exclusivity of pet ownership and the possibility that living with a pet does not really upset the boundary that has been erected between humans and animals. But here, however, something else emerges. Here the focus is not so much on how far the animals are transformed in their relationship with humans as on how far the humans are (or need to be) changed. In a sense we return to Nagel's argument about the limitations of the human, but we do so in ways that Nagel would find utterly alien.

For some pet owners a particularly strong kind of anthropomorphism is embraced in which the pet is positioned and referred to as a "fur baby" and the human owners regard themselves as "parents" to that "baby". Thus, for example, Jessica Greenebaum has studied the community of "fur babies" that meets every Thursday evening between 6 and 8 at Fido's Barkery (a bakery that sells only dog treats) in Hartford, Connecticut for "Yappy Hour". Here the dogs are allowed to play at the front of the shop while the humans enjoy a drink at the back. The "parents" regard themselves as being somehow different from other pet owners because they "take time out for their pets … [and do] something that's just specifically for their dog" (2004: 123). For them, regarding dogs as "fur babies" is an act of the greatest kindness because they believe that their pets have "attitude, needs, personality, thoughts" (*ibid.*: 122) like humans. Thus, in an interview with one young couple who attend

"Yappy Hour", and who are planning for their first child, the woman says of her dog, "Dakota will always be our first born" (*ibid.*: 129). In her mind difference does not exist because difference was never there in the first place. Her "fur baby" is just a baby with fur.

Here the pet is anthropomorphized because it is already believed to be human-like. And indeed anthropomorphism might be an unfair description of what takes place in the relationship with the "fur baby" because to argue that these "parents" are anthropomorphizing would be to suggest that they believe that they are transforming their pets, when in fact they would say, I think, that the pet does not need to be transformed; that it is always already simply a furry human. What does need to be transformed is our recognition of that fact. It is our human limitations (our relegation of animals to a lower status) that must be addressed.

Thus we can see played out in the concept of the "fur baby", I think, an extreme version of the human–pet relationship. What is central to that relationship is a belief that it is possible to comprehend what it is like to be a pet. This is vital to any human–pet relationship as such relationships can only be formed with a firm belief in the "personhood" (for want of a better term) of the animal. But in a different way from the conceptualization of dogs that takes place in Fido's Barkery – where the humanization of the animals seems to be experienced as complete by the "parents" – for many pet owners the emphasis placed on access to the pet's inner being might not lead to a recognition of the humanity of the animal but instead might challenge the superiority of the human as it might remind us that we are incapable of imagining fully what it is like to be a pet because of our own limitations.

Whatever perspective we take then – whether what might be called the strong anthropomorphism of the fur babies' parents, or the less strong, but still anthropomorphic, desire to communicate with and gain an understanding (however limited) of a pet – what emerges from this discussion of the animal mind is just how important our sense of it is in the relationship between humans and pets. If we cannot access an animal's mind then pet owner-ship becomes potentially meaningless, for without a mind for us to access (or for us to believe we can access) we cannot really say that a pet loves, as such a claim would be simply anthropomorphic, and we need pets to be able to love if we are to be able to claim that dog love really is a kind of love. We need pets to have minds in order for them to be pets.

We can see these webs of anthropomorphism that exist in human–pet relations being played out in a very different place from the philosophy of mind of Nagel and the self-reflexive contempla-tions of Coetzee. And once again, it is a novel that shows us most clearly some of the issues involved. Margaret Marshall Saunders' *Beautiful Joe* is a dog's "autobiography" written to remind readers of their duties to animals. It begins, "My name is Beautiful Joe, and I am a brown dog of medium size. I am not beautiful, and I am not a thoroughbred. I am only a cur" (1965: 9). This, of course, is utterly anthropomorphic; Beautiful Joe thinks, writes, understands like a human; he uses human categories (not beautiful, a cur) to define himself; he is, in fact, a furry human. The reason for this choice of narrative technique is simple: telling a story from the first-person perspective allows direct access to the innermost feelings of the central character. Thus, giving Beautiful Joe a voice and an interior-being elevates his status and reminds readers that animals also have selves: that there is something that it is like to be a dog. This was the didactic aim of *Beautiful Joe*, a novel that tells the story of a rescued dog that won the American Humane Education Society's competi-tion to find a canine *Black Beauty* in 1893.

But the anthropomorphism of Saunders's book inevitably turns around on itself. If Costello's claim that a bat should be considered as another human actually and also proclaims the omniscience of the human, Saunders' novel also shows how anthropomorphism can work against what it seems to achieve. *Beautiful Joe* is an attempt to encourage kinder treatment of animals but what it actually does is entirely cancel out the presence of the pet as animal and unravel the status of the human. This is made visible when Saunders has the dog report his human saviour Harry's statement that "Man is a god to the lower creation" (1965: 216). Placing this argument for dominion in the mouth of a dog makes it appear natural and true, just as Lassie's desire to come home made pet ownership seem natural and true. But in actuality, of course, what we are getting in *Beautiful Joe* are a human's (Harry's) words voiced by a dog (Beautiful Joe), which is itself a human construction (a fictional creation). As such, the declaration that humans are gods to animals might actually be saying something rather different from what initially appears to be the case, something that reveals the contradictions in many of our ways of thinking about pets. We might read the statement, indeed, as saying something along the lines of: we humans are constantly anxious about our status and so we do something utterly paradoxical to address this. We construct animals as beings like us in order to show how powerful we are in our control over them and simultaneously we make it appear that our power is natural in that it is given by animals that we have also constructed as instinctive and not rational. In such a narrative, we construct pets as both like us and not like us in order to reinforce and naturalize the fact that we are the only beings that really count in the world, all because we are anxious that that might not be true. In these terms, it could be argued that Harry saves Beautiful Joe from his cruel owner not because cruelty is wrong, or because the dog is harmed, but in order that Beautiful Joe might proclaim Harry's God-like status. And this would reveal, of course, how far humanist ideas about the human, which posit the superiority of humanity, rely on pets. Once again, it is them who make us.

But they undo us too. The possibility of humans accessing the mind of the animals they live with is fraught with difficulty. Animals – even those we know best – mark the end of our apparent omniscience. Humanist humanity is undone when the animal mind is contemplated, either because the animal mind is revealed to be just like the human mind, thus destroying notions of human superiority; or because the animal mind is recognized as being always beyond our understanding, thus revealing how limited that understanding actually is. Whichever way you approach the issue, what is revealed are the frailties of the human.

But what if we turn to the animal once again and recognize something else? Thus far we have been putting into human terms what animals do. What if we attempted to understand what animals mean *as animals*? The difference between an anthropomorphic engagement and one that attempts to interpret animals on their own terms is made visible in the central technique of *Beautiful Joe*: the fact that this is a dog's "autobiography". This self-recording, as I have said, reinforces the presence of Beautiful Joe as a self through anthropomorphism, but by giving Beautiful Joe a voice Saunders also allows a glimpse of what giving a voice might actually mean. Beautiful Joe recognizes something about human–pet relations that reminds us of the power structure inherent in those relations: "I don't believe human beings would love animals as well", he says, "if they could speak" (1965: 144). We like our pets' silence because it allows us to write their words for them, and what they say – what we write – reminds us of our power. Lassie tells us she wants to come home. Beautiful Joe tells us how grateful he is for human omniscience. But this, of course, is fantasy: real animals do "speak", even if they cannot write autobiographies. Numerous studies have shown that animals do have something that can be termed language (if we use that term in its broadest sense to refer to a system of communication). This is a fact that has been ignored in the discussions looked at so far, and we need to consider their ability to communicate with us not simply our possible failure to imagine them if we are to think fully about what it means to live with an animal.

The language of the pet

A dog stands before me; its ears are pricked, its shoulders lowered and its tail stands straight up. Should I stroke it and make eye contact, or keep my arms by my side and avert my gaze? A cat stands, tail held high, and head-butts my hand. Does it want me to move my hand away, or does it want me to tickle it? Almost anyone who has ever encountered a pet dog or cat will know the answers here, because almost anyone who has ever encountered a pet dog or cat has learned to read that animal's meaning. Language, after all, is not only spoken. And if we cannot work it out for ourselves there are shelves full of books available to help us. So, for example, in *How to Speak Dog*, Stanley Coren offers a "visual glossary" and a "doggish phrasebook" that might enable readers to interpret more fully their dog's language. He offers definitions of "sound signals" (barks, whines, growls) and also explains the meaning of "tail signals" (wagging, held low, held high), "ear signals", "eye signals" and so on. Coren's lexicon is constructed through observation and experience; he has learned to interpret the dogs he is watching and training. He reads their minds – their moods, their emotional states – because he has trained himself to interpret their outward actions.

Coren's ideal, however, isn't only that humans should learn to read dogs. If this was all he was interested in it would simply allow his readers to take up the position of observers in their relationships with their pets. Coren sees human–pet communication as two-way; we are observers and actors at the same time and, importantly, so are the pets. He proposes that humans should learn not only to read the language of dogs but to speak it as well in that we should pay attention to what they tell us and modify our own behaviour in order to avoid errors in communication that can take place. For example, a dog that is perceived to "smile" may actually be showing its teeth in annoyance, and so a human smiling back at that dog could simply be reinforcing the aggressive potential of such a confrontation. The irritated dog might understand itself as not being smiled at so much as challenged by an angry being and this could lead to a violent altercation. Recognizing the potential to misinterpret the dog's expression and the subsequent poor choice of human expression could (should) be the basis for a change in human behaviour that might avoid biting and the subsequent euthanizing of an apparently violent pet. Unlike in an English literature class, interpretation can be a matter of life and death in this context.

But the possibility of a cross-species conversation is not the only point being made here. We can read *How to Speak Dog* as having wider, more abstract implications for human–pet relations. Coren's model of communication reminds us, for example, that human language – even human body language, in which the smile is a friendly expression – is not the only language in the world. Indeed, Coren's terms for different ways of communicating with dogs reveal, once again, just how far a pet has the potential to undermine human concepts of human power. "Doggish" is the name he gives to the language of dogs, thus giving it an equivalent status to English, Spanish, Danish and so on (and by extension we could learn cattish, gerblish, hamstish). On the other hand, Coren recognizes that the spoken dialect humans often use to communicate with pets – like "Motherese", the language often used when addressing babies – has short sentences, exists primarily in the present tense and is full of repetition: "Rover, go pee. Go pee, Rover". This language Coren names "doggerel", the term for bad poetry.

His choice of word is appropriate. Not only is there a pleasing pun at work, but there is also – accidentally, perhaps, but aptly – a play on a concept of the human that has come down through classical philosophy. Following Aristotle's various conceptions of the special nature of the human – as the rational animal, the political animal, the only animal that laughs – philosophers have sought to outline what it is that distinguishes humans from the so-called lower creatures. Art has been used as a marker of difference: only humans can create art, the argument goes (and the interest in paintings by apes and elephants in recent years shows how significant and anxious-making such a claim remains). Indeed, the sixteenth-century scholar George Puttenham was so wedded to this idea that he argued in *The Arte of English Poesie* ([1589] 1970) that it was poetry that made us human: that without literature we would be mere savage beasts.

It is this alignment of poetry and the human that comes apart in Coren's use of the term "doggerel". Addressing an animal using only human language does not proclaim the power of the human as it might be supposed to do, for asserting the existence of only one language would seem to be an exercise in control and domination: something revealed by the history of colonial oppression. Rather, the language that is used when addressing a pet reveals just how foolish and disappointing such human power is: "Rover, go pee. Go pee, Rover" is hardly poetry and so hardly an adequate expression of our humanity. Thus *How to Speak Dog*, while not a philosophical text as such, invokes notions of human difference and superiority that are central to humanist conceptions of the human, and that remain so powerful in the twenty-first century, but it reveals them to be deeply flawed and arrogant. Inherent in the book, then, is a reminder that, rather than relying on our belief in animal incapacity (the belief that they cannot speak or write poetry), we must learn to recognize animal capacity and human limitation (that they do speak, it's just that we don't understand them). In short, we can speak doggerel to them if we wish (many pets are capable of learning some human terms after all), but we must also learn to speak doggish to begin to engage with them more fully. By implication we must abandon our belief in our status as separate and superior to them if we are to live successfully with our pets; a conversation must take place.

Abandoning ideas of human difference does not simply mean celebrating the similarities of humans and animals, however. This can lead to its own problems, as Elizabeth Costello's theory shows. What Coren's story of the "smiling" dog reminds us, for example, is that reading the animal as if it was just another (furry) human can lead to crucial errors. We make our pets like us (they live in our houses) and yet we must remember that, in crucial ways, they are not like us at all. Just as cats and dogs speak different languages (a cat's wagging tail signals aggression, a dog's is a sign of happiness), so the smile reminds us that humans and dogs are separated by a gulf of difference. And the fact that it can be a smile that makes this difference visible is good evidence to support literary scholar Alice A. Kuzniar's (2006) belief in the melancholy nature of human–dog relations. How can I warmly greet a dog if my warm greeting might be its cold irritation?

But Coren offers us a way of bridging the gulf between Costello's and Nagel's perspectives by offering clues as to the meaning of a dog even as he reminds us of the importance of acknowledging the difference between pet owners and pets. Anthropomorphic interpretations, such as the one that assumes that when a dog's mouth forms a shape that resembles a human smile it too is smiling, blank out difference and transform the world into the human. However, asserting that animals have language is giving them a status that is missing in anthropomorphic interpretations. They are not simply soundless symbols of human desires and human anxieties but active, communicating beings engaged in world-making alongside humans.

We need to pause, though. Undoubtedly Coren's study is an extremely useful tool in human–pet relations. But what his lexicon cannot necessarily give us is any insight into the animal's interior being: what it is like to be a pet. The lexicon can interpret outward actions and from them assert an inner state, but it does not really allow us access to what Thomas called the "hidden life" of dogs.

She, like Coren, attempted to find this by watching and interpreting her dogs' actions and, like Coren, was undoubtedly successful in many ways. But she also had to acknowledge, if implicitly, that there are some things in animals' minds that humans can never get at without potentially cancelling out some of the animal-ness of the animal; that anthropomorphism – transforming pet into human – prowls at the margins. In translation, doggish can be rewritten to say things that it might not have said in the original. This not only takes the form of mistaking an angry grimace for a smile, but it also lurks in another form in the doggish lexicon itself. Experience has taught Coren that a dog that appears to smile may not be smiling at all but may be annoyed. However, Coren is not really able to assert what it is he might mean by the term "annoyed" when it is applied to a being that is not human. What is canine irritation like for the dog? We know what it might result in – headlines are still made when dogs attack humans – but we really don't know what it is that the dog experiences.

Thus learning to speak doggish may not actually be enough. Even if we are correct when we assert that a pet is happy – on the return of its owner after her absence, to have the freedom of an open space after a day of confinement – we cannot truly know whether a pet's experience of happiness is just the same as what we mean when we use the word "happy" to define a state that we experience. Is cat bliss the same as human bliss? Masson puts the issue succinctly:

> In the case of dogs, their emotional responses so resemble our own that we are tempted to assume identity; the joy of a dog appears to be identical to human joy, the sorrow of a dog the same as our sorrow. Yet we can never claim that we know precisely what a dog feels. The joy and sorrow of dogs are canine joys and sorrows and may differ from our own feelings in ways too subtle to recognize or articulate. (1997: xv–xvi)

This problem is exacerbated when one confronts species with emotional responses less outwardly recognizable than dogs'. Rats, rabbits, guinea pigs, hamsters, snakes and lizards: all these animals are sentient beings, capable of engaging with the world in their own ways, and have abilities to communicate with other members of their own species, and – if only in limited ways – with humans (this is why we like them as pets). I would not want to deny that they also all possess the capacity to feel pain and experience pleasure, but what is snake delight? How does a gerbil experience enjoyment? A dedicated pet owner needs to have some idea of an answer to these kinds of questions if he or she is to offer the animal the fullest and happiest life possible. Not being able to come up with any answers would seem to make pet ownership utterly selfish in that, without a concept of animal pleasure, it must concern itself completely with the only knowable pleasure: that of the human. Without knowledge of pet joy, pet ownership would be utterly anthropocentric, and dog love always only really human love in disguise.

Coren's *How to Speak Dog* and books like it are one attempt to construct the interior life of the animal and allow for the concept of animal pleasure. By writing a phrasebook based on careful observations and by collecting anecdotal evidence Coren is able to make claims about how dogs experience the world. And he is not alone in making such claims about animals. In their study of the behaviour of cats in a cat shelter, for example, sociologists Janet M. Alger and Steven F. Alger argue that "there are many indications that the otherness of nonhuman animals is not impenetrable" (1999: 201). Ethnographic research, they note, shows how important nonverbal communication is in human interaction, and so it is no great stretch to recognize animals' body language as also communicating meaning. Such communication works in two ways: not only do the cats read human signals – "Beckoning is recognized as meaning" – but they also make their own signs, making "demands based on successful past interactions" (*Ibid.*).

But such recognition that there is something that can be read in animal language does not address the deeper problem. Coren, like many psychologists and sociologists, applies human criteria that put an end to further discussion about the nature of an animal. The assumption Coren makes is that a dog's irritation is enough like a human's to not warrant further discussion, and there are good reasons for this assumption. Firstly, as Alger and Alger write, "it can be counter-productive to emphasize unduly the differences between us and those companion animals with whom we have such a long history of inter-species communication" (*ibid.*: 202). Perhaps it is possible that a cat's experience of bliss is like a human's and that concerns about the difference between humans and their pets actually hide the reality that there are important similarities. What we dismiss as anthropomorphic may not be anthropomorphic at all. And indeed, dismissing what can be recognized as animals' apparently human-like behaviour as merely evidence of our anthropomorphic tendencies (which are often regarded as sentimental) could be evidence of the "disavowal" of animals that Wolfe proposed as central to the ways in which our humanity is constructed. It would be dangerous to a concept of the human as utterly distinct and separate from animals if we believed that animals acted like humans. And so representing anything that presents animals' actions in human terms as "merely" anthropomorphic reinforces species difference. It implies that a proper – a less sentimental – vision would recognize how very different (and implicitly inferior) animals really are.

The second reason why we should follow Coren and assume that dog irritation is like human irritation is because it would be something of a philosophical dead-end to attempt to come up with a concept that expressed the difference between canine and human irritation. Not only can we never really know what a pet feels because it is an animal, but also any terms that we might construct to define animal actions that avoided humanization would still be human terms. We cannot get away from ourselves. There is a

creature knows exactly where it is at every waking moment [because the] animal brain carries its own global positioning device. (Quoted in Steeves 2005: 29)

Such a statement would seem to present a positive image of animal capacity, but Pyle's statement is actually yet another rendition of humanism: yet another relegation of the animal to a lower strata. H. Peter Steeves writes in response to Pyle: "I want to resist thinking – even metaphorically – that animals are fleshy technology … It leads to no good" (*ibid*.: 30). The "no good" that Steeves is referring to here is, among other things, Descartes's classing of animals as mere automata, which Steeves argues provides a foundation for Pyle's claim. To assert, as Pyle does, that animals have an inbuilt GPS is not to celebrate the natural capacity of animals so much as it is to consign animals to the status of machines: "To say that the animal cannot be lost is to strip her of a home. … To say that the animal cannot be lost is to strip him of a will" (*ibid*.: 30–31).

The implications of this reading of the animal as machine are terrifying; most famously Descartes argued that animals cannot feel pain because they do not have the capacity to think – do not possess what he called the "*cogitatio*" – that is required for such an experience. John Cottingham summarizes Descartes' position in a way that allows him to account for the fact that an animal can certainly appear to be hurt (it can yelp, yowl, howl and so on). He writes, "I should certainly say that cats feel pain, but not that they have the kind of full mental awareness of pain that is needed for it to count as a *cogitatio*" (1978: 558). For followers of Descartes, a cat's pain is less painful than a human's pain because, while a cat can respond to a painful stimulus – it would leap away from a fire, for example – the underlying reason for the cat's leap would be different from a human's because the experience of the burning would be different. Pain, for Descartes, is a cognitive event and animals do not have the rational capacities that humans have, and therefore they do not feel pain like humans. A history of human dominion – in experimental practices, meat-eating, farming – emerges from and finds support in such a concept of animal lack, even as that lack – as in Pyle's notion of the animal's inbuilt GPS – appears to be a benefit.

The model of animal capacity as a mechanical one works in direct opposition to the previous one I have outlined. Descartes does not attempt to comprehend animal language using human concepts (Coren's proposal); rather, he bases his argument on the belief that animals have no language at all. For him this is the key to knowing that they do not have the cognitive capacity to experience the world as more than machines. All humans, Descartes writes, are capable of "arranging various words together and forming an utterance from them in order to make their thoughts understood; whereas there is no other animal … that can do the like" (1985: 140). He denies that this is due to animals' physical differences from humans (their lack of appropriate organs for speech), but argues that their lack of language shows "not merely that beasts have less reason than men, but that they have no reason at all. For it patently requires very little reason to speak" (*ibid.*).

Animal languages are ignored by Descartes because they are not perceived as languages at all, but as series of noises – barks, mews, squawks and chirps – made in reaction to the existence of particular external stimuli, and because of this animals are believed to be mere automata. A wagging tail in this system does signify, but what it signifies is simply the dog's status as fleshy machine. The wagging tail is a mechanical exhibition of joy: a bliss response, you might say, not evidence of the experience of bliss itself. This is, to say the least, a partial argument; an assumption has been made (by a human) that language is human and it is from this position that a theory has been built. It may not be anthropomorphic – indeed, it is the absolute opposite of anthropomorphism – but Descartes's philosophy is certainly, like anthropomorphism, putting the human first.

Derrida offers a helpful outline of Descartes's interpretation of language, an interpretation that he wants to challenge. He traces its persistence in the writings of the twentieth-century psychoanalyst Jacques Lacan and summarizes Lacan's analysis as follows: "When bees appear to 'respond' to a 'message,' [Lacan argues,] they do not respond but react; they merely obey a fixed program, whereas the human subject responds to the other, to the question posed by the other" (2003: 125). The opposition Derrida sets up here between a reaction and a response is a reiteration of the difference between a mechanical and what we might call an emotional experience of the world. An animal reacts, just as a clock will tell the time, not because it understands but because it is simply constructed to do this. Humans, on the other hand, respond; they engage with the world as thinking beings, capable of giving individually mean-ingful answers to individually meaningful questions. Humans are not trapped in the regularity of a clockwork existence, they have choices, and thus they make responses.

The essay Derrida writes in reply to Lacan (and all those other philosophers who assume a direct link between language and humanity) poses a challenge. It is entitled "And Say the Animal Responded?". What would philosophers do, Derrida is asking, if animals were perceived as being capable of communicating (responding) like humans? How would that change the way we under-stand the world and our relationship to it? Using Coren's work we can glimpse some possible answers to such questions in that it shows us how some of the assumptions that underpin humanist ideas might be undone if we accept the existence of doggish and doggerel. In the first instance, recognizing the existence of animal language reveals, once again, humans' ability to interpret animals to be limited; we cannot fully know all that they are saying. In the second instance, human language itself is revealed to be limited in that it cannot represent the many beings with which it shares the world. Either way, human power is undercut when the animal is believed to respond.

I began this chapter asking what the declaration that dog love is love would entail: what it would mean to human–pet relations if we do firmly believe that the relationship with a pet is a real relationship and not just a fake one in which the animal stands in for an absent human. I would argue that, if dog love is love, the dog must have within it the capacity to be loved and must reciprocate – respond – with something that can also be called love. If this is the case then pet owners need their pets to have interior lives for the relationship between the pet and the human to be more than either only symbolically meaningful (the dog constructing a comforting concept of the human home) or egocentric (our pleasure being the only pleasure). Understanding something of an animal's language is one way of accessing the inner being of the animal, but this is not just about learning the doggish phrasebook; it is also about acknowledging that there is something that it is like to be an animal. To read doggish is to open up the possibility of communication with another species that is not flattening out difference but celebrating it. But making the leap across the species barrier brings with it difficulties. How do we know we are getting it right? How do we know we are not transforming the dog's meaning into a human meaning? These questions are unanswerable, but the implications of not making the leap are potentially horrendous and would kill any possibility that dog love is love. And so we make our educated guesses, we acknowledge that our knowledge is limited but that it is the best we have.

So how do we move forwards from here? The possibility of communication across species boundaries – however poor that communication might be – does remind us both how different humans are from their pets (we cannot really speak their language even after years of cohabitation) and how, even with this acknowledged limitation, it is possible to bridge the gap between pet and owner (we can learn some doggish, they can learn some doggerel). And it is these two things – difference and bridging the gap – that we need to have in place simultaneously when we think about living with animals. We need to find an ethics for human–pet relations that does not assume that being like a human is the only possible subject status, but that accepts the animal-ness of the animal if we are ever going to establish that it is possible that dog love really is love.

The love of the pet

In a defence of his philosophical position on animals Descartes argued that "my opinion is not so much cruel to animals as indulgent to human beings … since it absolves them from the suspicion of crime when they eat or kill animals" (1985: vol. III, 366). This sounds absurd. How can a theory that proclaims that animals cannot experience pain not be cruel to those animals? The reason is simple: in Descartes's theory one can only be cruel to a being with the cognitive capacity to experience it. Any moral stricture against the mistreatment of animals in this framework can only be based on criteria like the animal's property value (kicking a dog being the equivalent to scratching a car) and so the suffering of the animal is dismissed.

What is visible in Descartes's notion of cruelty is a sense in which subject status and ethical status are linked. This is a belief repeated by Coetzee's Elizabeth Costello with very different intentions. If we declare a bat to have the same status as "another human" then clearly we can also assume that that bat is capable – as we assume a human is – of experiencing pain. This leap from bat to human to a shared experience of pain is an imaginative one: Costello believes that she has the ability to conceive of what it was like to be "a bat or a chimpanzee or an oyster, any being with whom I share the substrate of life" (1999b: 35). But Costello is not the first person to make a connection between the imagination and an ethical relationship with another being, and we see in a very different construction of this link a way forward that offers, perhaps, a middle ground between Nagel's melancholy refusal to believe and Costello's reductive assertion that one can comprehend what it is like to be a bat.

For Costello imagination allows for sympathy for the other, but for philosopher Nancy E. Snow it is our ability to be *compassionate* that rests on our imagination. Compassion and sympathy are both what Snow terms "other-regarding" emotions, but compassion, she argues, is "a 'suffering with' another" while sympathy, although similar, can be a response to less serious circumstances: "we sympathize with someone whose car has been scratched or who suffers from indigestion, but we would not ordinarily feel … compassion for that person" (1991: 197). Snow argues that it is through "imaginative dwelling", through putting oneself "in the other's place", that compassion exists: "The ability to identify with another's distress makes the other's suffering real to those who feel compassion, and facilitates benevolent desires for the other's good" (*ibid.*). For her the key to compassion is identification: our ability to think to ourselves as we witness another being experiencing, say, pain, "that could be me". Thus, I see someone fall off their bike and feel for them because I identify with them as I know what it is like to have such an accident, and from that "feeling for", that "suffering with", I offer help and attempt to make right what is a wrong not to me but to a fellow being who I imagine is like me. This is compassion, and it is an imaginative response to the world. A person who could not imagine themselves into the suffering of another would not feel for or suffer with that person: would not be compassionate but might be a psychopath.

Snow is not writing specifically about compassion for animals, but it is possible to see how in her model compassion could be felt for a member of another species. When contemplating compassion we are constantly reminded that we can really only experience our own experiences. Compassion works, after all, by a constant reference to the self: I feel for you because I understand myself and

I imagine that you are like me. In compassion, as in anthropomorphism, I am central to my relationship to the rest of the world. But compassion, while it may make the world self-like, does not make the relationship to the rest of the world inherently selfish. It is by recognizing that I am simultaneously different from and yet similar to other beings in the world that compassion works: I don't writhe around on the ground in pain when you fall off your bike but I can imagine that your pain might not be any differently painful from the pain that I have experienced. It is an imaginative leap in that I cannot prove that your pain and my pain are the same, but nor do I want to try to do that. My imaginative leap is, somehow, beyond proof and I respond to the suffering of another without the need for such corroboration.

Such understanding of compassion raises an important possibility for pet owners, for, indeed, what is pet ownership if it is not itself a form of "imaginative dwelling", the phrase Snow uses to define compassion. In this sense, inviting an animal into one's home is already something like an act of compassion. But there are other ways of viewing the relationship with the pet as a potentially compassionate one. If there is no sense of proof involved in my compassionate response to another human (your experience of pain, and even your expression of that experience, may be nothing like my own) then I can easily see a way in which such imagining could be extended to read, however provisionally, the experience of an animal. Thus the step from feeling for another human to feeling for another animal is not as great as it might appear to be. I would not want to go as far as Elizabeth Costello and assert that, say, a hamster should be understood "as another human" (what is wrong with a hamster being a hamster?), and nor do I think a concept of cat "joy" is anything but problematic. But assuming the presence of another consciousness need not require us to fully comprehend the nature of that consciousness because it is possible that we do not actually understand any consciousnesses apart from our own anyway and, after Freud, of course, we know we rarely even understand that. We do not have to know what it is like to be a dog to know that there is a being called a dog that is able perhaps only tentatively to communicate with us. And we need this tentative communication to be understood as communication – as a response and not just a reaction – because if we take a bark to be a meaningless noise or a feline head-butt to be an aggressive gesture we are refusing to engage with the animal and that is something that pet ownership requires of us.

Thus pet ownership, like compassion, requires imagination. To bring an animal into one's home, to live with it as a member of the family, is not simply to ignore difference; it is to engage in an ongoing process of translation. It is to make educated guesses that rely on both empirical observation (watching how an animal responds) and imagination. A thought that begins "If I was a cat ..." could be relegated to the realm of "mere" anthropomorphism, but it is also a productive – not to say compassionate – mode of cohabitation.

And there is another analogy, I think, that is helpful here. If compassion is based not on a full experience of the pain of another being but an imaginative one, we can see that reading fiction might be a model of compassion. Many novelists ask their readers to care: to put themselves in the situation of the characters; to feel the horror or joy felt by a character. In *Midnight's Children*, for example, Salman Rushdie's storyteller Saleem Sinai states at one point "I have not, I think, been good at describing emotions – believing my audience to be capable of *joining in*; of imagining, for themselves, what I have been unable to re-imagine, so that my story becomes yours as well" (2006: 408). This is highly self-conscious on Rushdie's part, but it says something important about our relationship with the world around us and it reminds us that our power to author – to create – that world is limited. But it also says something about the process of reading; without "joining in" we readers would simply be observing the world we were reading about and not engaged with it (of course, this can be a relationship between reader and text that some writers, Bertolt Brecht, for example, would prefer). Just as Coren proposed that we need to both read and speak doggish, so *engaging* with fiction, not just reading it, can affect us more. Fiction calls up compassion even as it takes us out of reality, and the two are not in opposition because compassion itself is an act of imaginative reading.

But literature has another role to play. In its methods of representation literary texts can also be regarded as laying bare the world in that they have the potential to show things in ways that jolt us out of our everyday perceptions. Writing in the early twentieth century the Russian critic Roman Jakobson argued that literary writing is an "organized violence committed on ordinary speech"; that it "defamiliarizes" the world by making the commonplace seem strange again (quoted in Eagleton 1983: 2). One representation of how this works comes from another Russian author, Victor Shklovsky: art, he argued, "makes the stone stony" (quoted in Lodge 1988: 20). That is, in representing something as ordinary as a stone, art has the capacity to make us look at that stone in new ways; it has the capacity to make us experience the stony-ness that has been forgotten with familiarity. If such is taken as one of its key techniques then it can be seen that literature can lead us to a reassessment of the world, which can, in turn, lead to a reconnection with it. Literature, in short, can lead to a reactivation of compassion for that which has been deadened by familiarity.

And we can bring all of this together. If pet ownership, like compassion, requires imagination, then clearly literature that focuses on pets might have something particularly important to say. Perhaps it is not just that novelists happen to be insightful about pets (my argument in the previous chapter); perhaps it is *because* they are novelists – are *imaginative* writers – that they are insightful. It might be that all of the problems that I have traced in this chapter are about reading. Thus, accessing an animal's inner life (what it is like to be an animal) is an act of the imagination. The attempt to have a conversation across the species barrier is not so different from the act of interpretation that is often involved in reading novels, which tell of lives not our own. Feeling compassion for and loving an animal is making an imaginative leap that is also like that required of us by many novelists. We connect with what is inaccessible by engaging ourselves in the process of understanding.

I want to turn finally to show how all of the possibilities and problems of literary representation can be traced in one particular work in a way that reflects the concerns of this chapter. In *Flush* (1933), a fictional biography of the nineteenth-century poet Elizabeth Barrett Browning's pet spaniel, Virginia Woolf imagines poet and dog's first meeting, and it is worth quoting at length to get a sense of her representation of the human–pet relation here:

> Each was surprised. Heavy curls hung down on either side of Miss Barrett's face; large bright eyes shone out; a large mouth smiled. Heavy ears hung down on either side of Flush's face; his eyes, too, were large and bright; his mouth was wide. There was a likeness between them. As they gazed at each other each felt: Here am I – and then each felt: But how different! Hers was the pale worn face of an invalid, cut off from the air, light, freedom. His was the warm ruddy face of a young animal; instinct with health and energy. Broken asunder, yet made in the same mould, could it be that each completed what was dormant in the other? She might have been – all that; and he – But no. Between them lay the widest gulf that can separate one being from another. She spoke. He was dumb. She was woman; he was dog. (1998: 18–19)

The mode of representation that Woolf uses is deliberately incoherent. There is anthropomorphism ("each felt: Here am I"), but there is also its opposite, the closing off of similarity ("She spoke. He was dumb"). There is closeness ("likeness") and there is separation ("the widest gulf").

The relationship with the pet, for Woolf, seems to include all of these things; hence it is a relationship that cannot be captured by the hygiene of human concepts and so incoherence, paradoxically, is a logical response. For Woolf this realization also includes a very self-conscious recognition that, as such, the pet will always escape our ability to represent it in anything but the most limited, partial ways. Indeed, when she attempts to discuss Flush's experience of the world Woolf offers two possibilities. The first, early in the novel, shows the impossible nature of representing what it is to be a dog using human language. Flush is exploring Miss Barrett's room:

> That huge object by the window was perhaps a wardrobe. Next to it stood, conceivably, a chest of drawers. In the middle of the room swam up to the surface what seemed to be a table with a ring round it; and then the vague amorphous shapes of armchair and table emerged. (*Ibid.*: 16)

"Perhaps", "conceivably", "seemed", "vague": Woolf deliberately places her ability to describe what the dog sees under the scrutiny of doubt. She simultaneously describes the room for us, her human readers, and shows how a dog could never know that what it saw was a wardrobe, a chest of drawers, and so on, because such objects are human. In doing this Woolf reminds us that our presence in and perception of the world are not the only ones.

Towards the end of the novel, however, when poet and dog have moved to Italy (and, once again, a link is made between the dog coming home and the transformation of the home in *Flush*) Woolf uses another method to represent Flush's experience. Acknowledging the centrality of the sense of smell to the dog's being in the world, Woolf resorts to synaesthetic descriptions to capture how that world might be to reading (not scenting) humans. That is, she uses impossible concepts that overlay the human understanding with the canine one by using sensory experience from one organ to describe the experience of another. Running around, Flush scents "raucous smells, crimson smells": he loves grapes because of their "purple smell", and "knew Florence as no human being has ever known it ... Not a single one of his myriad sensations ever submitted itself to the deformity of words" (*ibid.*: 87). The irony is, of course, that it is only in the deforming of description – the use of synaesthesia – that Woolf can make this point. But it is important that it is not only Flush's experience that is potentially deformed in language: Woolf has just said of his owner, the great poet herself, "She could not find words enough in the whole of the English language to express what she felt" (*ibid.*: 85). If a poet cannot find the words to express her own experience, Woolf silently seems to ask, how can we possibly ever hope to express what a dog feels? The problem of "What is it Like to be a Bat?" becomes the problem of "What is it Like to be a Human?". So alongside the acknowledgement of the "widest gulf" between human and canine in *Flush* is something else; if humans – even poets – cannot find the words, how different are we from dogs after all?

Thus the acknowledgement of the difference between humans and animals is not melancholy for Woolf. In *Flush* the realization of human limitation is something to be celebrated in playful prose, and difficulties of representation and comprehension do not close off the possibility of friendship but rather reveal new ways of being and cohabiting in the world. "Thus closely united, thus immensely divided", Woolf writes, "they gazed at each other. Then with one bound Flush sprang onto the sofa and laid himself where he was to lie for ever after – on the rug at Miss Barrett's feet" (*ibid.*: 19). Here, we might say, is dog love.

4. Being with pets

The dog here is at the feet of the human and thus if the relationship between Elizabeth Barrett and Flush is dog love, then dog love appears to include both dominance and submission. And if this is the case, can this really be a vision of love? Should we, rather, recognize Woolf's representation of Flush's agency – his desire to be at his mistress's feet (rather like Lassie's desire to come home) – as simply another idealization of human power by a human: another veiling of domination? Or should we read this image of Flush at the feet of his mistress as an acknowledgement that such hierarchy can, in fact, be love? Is this the best that we can hope for? Is dog love – as Tuan might have it – always a blend of dominance and affection?

I want to attempt in this chapter to trace whether we might be able to live with pets without asserting dominance over them and what the philosophical and ethical implications of such living might be. So far in this book I have offered an account of living with pets that seems constantly to veer in a very different direction. I have argued how easy it is to cancel out the presence of the real animal and instead use its symbolic possibilities. I then considered what thinking about the nature of the pet might offer to the pet owner and traced the difficulties of knowing what it is that one is living with, and why it is so important to assume – imagine – such knowledge. In different ways earlier chapters have, I hope, made clear what complex beings pets are for humans: how they simultaneously breach and reconstruct boundaries; how they reveal both human fragmentation and human power; how we speak to them and show the inadequacies of our modes of communication; how they speak to us and reveal our inability to understand. In all of this Franklin's claim that pets provide "ontological security" in a fractured world seems difficult to uphold. And yet he must be right, for if pets did simply uproot, challenge, test and disrupt it seems unlikely that so many households would include them; it seems implausible that they could be so loved. And they are loved. Against all the odds – ignoring the communication difficulties, financial outlay, smell, hair, faeces, piss, noise, demands – many humans love their pets. Perhaps it is because all these difficulties persist that the pet is so significant. Perhaps if it was easy to have a mutual relationship the dog sitting at one's feet would be less meaningful.

But this would be to accept that sitting at the feet of the owner is the only possible conception of the pet's place in the home. It would be to assume that at the heart of human–pet relations there persists a hierarchy that supports human dominance. In this chapter I want, as I have said, to explore some alternatives. I shall begin by thinking about why dogs have figured so heavily in this book so far. Central to the focus on dogs is, I think, a naturalized assumption about how humans live with animals more generally. This is an assumption that has its roots in a philosophical tradition that needs to be more fully explored than it has been so far, and is an assumption that might be challenged if another animal – a cat – is considered as the philosophical exemplar of the pet. I shall trace the differences between dogs and cats not through clichés about the difference between dog lovers and cat lovers (although they are not unconnected to this debate) but through an analysis of the philosophical discourses that use each animal to represent what it means to think and be human. A philosophy that thinks with cats, I suggest, might be a different kind of philosophy to the one that thinks with dogs.

Having thought about cats, however, I want to return to dogs and read an alternative theorization about what it can mean to live with a dog. I shall trace another understanding of human–pet relations that not only offers a different set of terms, but also might take us beyond the conception of pet love that situates the dog at the feet of the human. I will suggest that perhaps, after all, it is not only cats that can be used to challenge orthodox ways of thinking. Finally, I return to the home and think through yet another model of living with animals that both takes seriously and challenges many of the assumptions that have been considered so far in this book. This time I am not thinking about dogs or cats, but about rabbits, and will raise questions about another way of living with an animal, and another way of being human.

As distinct from Chapters 2 and 3 this chapter is organized around the work of three key thinkers: Jacques Derrida, Donna Haraway and Julie Ann Smith. The reason for this focus is that I think that these writers are all responding to key ideas that have already been discussed in this book, and in their responses they offer three distinct glimpses of alternative ways of thinking and living with animals. I hope that by tracing their arguments we can begin to see not only how much further to go there might be in living with, thinking with and being with pets, but also how contemplating life with animals opens up some key issues in contemporary philosophy. Here, indeed, I would argue, is a true form of cohabitation: this is not only philosophers thinking about pets, but also pets allowing philosophers to think about thinking.

But I begin with a question that has been, perhaps, lurking quietly in the corner of this book: why has the focus been so much on dogs? This focus is my own, certainly, but it is also to be found in much of the material I have been looking at. The reason for the focus on dogs is not only that dogs have been popular pets since the beginnings of modern pet keeping (although that is certainly true). It is also that dogs can be read as having been central to a particular, and particularly influential, philosophical tradition. From this perspective, to think about other animals is to think about other ways of thinking.

The challenge of the pet

The image of the dog sitting at the feet of its owner – the vision of dog love that Virginia Woolf offers in *Flush* – has a history that links dog love directly with philosophy. An anonymous portrait from a fifteenth-century French manuscript, for example, shows a woman writing with a small white dog at her feet. The woman is Christine de Pisan (b. 1365), author of *The Book of the City of Ladies*, a text that began the first extended debate about the nature of women, known as the *querelle des femmes*. The dog in this image should not be interpreted as a lapdog, a symbol of the writer's femininity; rather, this dog, I think, places Christine in a lineage of male philosophers, as such scholars were often represented with a dog at their feet in Medieval and Renaissance iconography. Albrecht Dürer's 1514 woodcut "Saint Jerome in his Study" is probably the most famous version of this idea.

The dog in these pictures is not only (or even) a pet. It is a conventional symbol of philosophy. Writing in the fourth century the philosopher Basil the Great offered a parallel that reveals how this image works:

Pursuing his quarry and finding that the tracks part in different directions, the dog examines the tracks, and with little trouble he works out his syllogistic reasoning. The prey, he reasons, has escaped either hither or thither, or in a quite different direction, and since it is neither here nor there, only one direction remains. Thus, by eliminating the erroneous alternatives, the dog discloses the truth. So do also those grave men of thought, who, seated in front of geometrical figures, draw lines in the sand and, confronted with three propositions, have to discard two in order to discover the truth of the one that remains. (Quoted in Reuterswärd 1991: 211)

The tracking dog, first discussed by the philosopher Chrysippus (*c*.280–*c*.206 BCE), is, for Basil, a figure of the truth seeker; it is a symbol of those schools of philosophy that claim the possibility of retrieving absolute knowledge. Sitting at the philosopher's feet in iconography, the dog's skills are paralleled with the human's: the philosopher, albeit figuratively, sniffs towards the truth.

But while there is an analogy between dog and thinker, central to the idea of such philosophical certainty – the tracking of truth – is a sense of the absolute difference between humans and all other animals. Humans have reason, this argument goes, and can rationally contemplate the world. Animals, on the other hand, have no reason and live only in the realm of instinct and sense. The scenting dog should thus be read as a simile: the dog is *like* a scenting philosopher but it is not a philosopher. As well as this, the image is also a naturalization of philosophical enquiry: it suggests that we do with our minds rationally what dogs do with their bodies instinctively. Thus the image reveals the difference between humans and animals as the dog's "reasoning" is not based on a logical deduction so much as a sensory one. In two ways, then, Basil reinforces human status and its relation to a particular kind of philosophy. First, it reminds us that humans think whereas dogs scent (we are mind, they are body). This closes down the possibility of the rational animal. And secondly, the parallel of dog and philosopher reminds us that, as the dog hunting its quarry shows that the quarry exists (how else would a scent trail be left?) and thus can be (although isn't always) caught, so for the thinker the truth exists and is attainable (although is not always found). Basil's image, which is part of a wider tradition, links human status inalienably to one kind of philosophy. Engaging in rational enquiry leading to the discovery of truth is being human.

But not all philosophers believed in this correlation of human status and the discovery of philosophical truth, and an alternative tradition offers a different perspective on the possibilities of human knowledge. One of its most famous moments we have already come across: Michel de Montaigne's question about his games with his cat, "When I play with my cat, who knows if I am not a pastime to her more than she is to me?" This question sets up in the most homely terms an important philosophical issue, and the issue's seriousness is not undermined by its homeliness, by its presence in a scene in which a human and an animal, he writes, "entertain each other with reciprocal monkey tricks" (2003: 401). In fact, the seriousness is, I would argue, enhanced by its domesticity: it is the very day-to-dayness of Montaigne's contemplation that makes it valuable.

Montaigne's question about his cat comes directly after the following assertion about the nature of human superiority (and note that even in the late-sixteenth century the human imagination is figured as central to discussions about human–animal relations):

> It is by the vanity of this same imagination that [man] equals himself to God, attributes to himself divine characteristics, picks himself out and separates himself from the horde of other creatures, carves out their shares to his fellows and companions the animals, and distributes among them such portions of faculties and powers as he sees fit. How does he know, by the force of his intelligence, the secret internal stirrings of animals? By what comparison between them and us does he infer the stupidity that he attributes to them? (*Ibid.*)

"How does he know?" This question is key to Montaigne's philosophy. He later adds not an answer, but another question: "When I play with my cat, who knows if I am not a pastime to her more than she is to me?"

But why does Montaigne remove us from philosophical abstraction – the nature of the human imagination – and take us to this scene of a man playing with his cat? There is more to it than Montaigne offering an alternative to the image of the dog at the philosopher's feet. First, I think, he is moving deliberately from abstract (the nature of imagination) to concrete (playing with his cat) because it is his belief that it is only in the real world that the nature of animals and humans can be properly contemplated: symbolic animals have no place in his argument as they are always already human constructions. Secondly, he is proposing that pets are significant and appropriate tools for contemplation and should not be dismissed by philosophy and philosophers: "in my opinion", he writes later in this discussion, "if anyone studies closely what we see ordinarily of the animals that live among us, there is material there for him to find facts just as wonderful as those that we go collecting in remote countries and centuries" (*ibid.*: 416). Thirdly, and most significantly, Montaigne distinguishes himself from the ideas of theorists such as Aristotle and his followers who claim to be able to know things absolutely. Instead Montaigne presents knowledge as tentative and relative: he is a sceptic. In *Outlines of Scepticism* (second century CE), a text that was a great influence on Montaigne, Sextus Empiricus labelled Aristotelian philosophy "dogmatic" and wrote that "Those who are called Dogmatists in the proper sense of the word think that they have discovered the truth" (2000: 3). The pun in Dogmatism is accidental but apposite here and it is apt that Montaigne – the anti-Dogmatist – should not have a dog lying at his feet but a cat that he plays with, and that he believes might also be playing with him.

But why a cat? What is it that a cat offers to Montaigne and his philosophy that a dog cannot? We should bear in mind that Montaigne has no interest in symbolism; he really is thinking about a real cat. The answer is surprisingly simple, I think, and persists today in some of the clichés repeated about the difference between dogs and cats. If a dog is trainable, then a cat is much less easily tamed; it is a much more independent – less homely – animal. Indeed, rather than *constructing* the domestic sphere a cat might well be understood to challenge it: it is, indeed, in his interaction with his cat that Montaigne is brought to contemplate his own (lack of) power. Franklin sums up this perception of cats as it persists into modern thinking when he writes that they "are in but not of the social, and have been attributed with characteristics consistent with that. Cats are mysterious, secretive, sexual (female), aloof, intellectual, independent and spiritual; they are of nature whereas dogs are of culture" (1999: 101). They are, he continues "seen as independent and single minded (whereas dogs are more conservative and conforming)" (*ibid.*). Kathleen Kete goes so far as to call the cat "the anti-pet par excellence" (1994: 56). Similarly, philosopher and animal trainer Vicki Hearne (to whom I return) states that "Cats, unlike horses and dogs, are more likely in domestic situations (hanging around the house) to force the dimmest of us temporarily at least to abandon our epistemological heavy-handedness" (2000: 240).

Our limited knowledge of the universe – what Hearne calls "our epistemological heavy-handedness" – is challenged by a cat's refusal to be absorbed into our worldview. Hearne writes of her cat, Gumbie, for example, "her relationship to the world is mediated through mine only insofar as that mediation is congruent with the revolving 'I Am' that is Gumbie" (*ibid.*). We can see, I think, that a cat's refusal to conform to human expectations and desires makes it the ideal pet for philosophers to contemplate as they challenge the assurances of the dogmatic tradition. Christine de Pisan and Saint Jerome are attempting to retrieve philosophical certainties with their dogs at their feet, and these are certainties that persist in a humanist myth of living with a dog that we have already encountered: "When they had had Lassie", Joe Carraclough thought: "the home had been comfortable and warm and fine and friendly. Now that she was gone nothing went right. So the answer was simple. If Lassie were only back again, then everything once more would be as it used to be."

In myth and in philosophy, the dog brings clarity. The cat, however, offers something very different. In philosopher Hélène

Cixous's short story "The Cat's Arrival", the narrator asks, "Who would have thought that a united and harmonious family would end up sinking because it had run into a cat's back?" (2006: 27). Cats seem to disdain humans in a way that dogs do not: they are not pack animals; they are nocturnal in habit. Dogs on the other hand can be trained to become part of the human family, to live by its rules. Dogs, so this argument goes, do not force us to abandon our knowledge of the world.

For a sceptic like Montaigne, who doubts whether the human imagination can be anything but anthropocentric, who wonders what if anything can be really known, a discussion of the nature of human knowledge takes the form of questions: what do I know? How do I know it? These are questions asked of the most homely as well as the most abstract issues. "What do I know about my cat?" is inseparable from a meditation on the nature of human knowledge itself. Indeed, animals are central to scepticism because it is when we confront the non-human that human power so clearly unravels. What the sceptics recognized that dogmatic philosophers overlooked was that there are things that are beyond the comprehension of the human mind: as Sextus Empiricus wrote, "even if we do not understand the sounds of the so-called irrational animals, it is nevertheless not unlikely that they do converse and we do not understand them" (2000: 21). The double negative here – "not unlikely" – seems an utterly appropriate grammatical form for a sceptic: it is hesitant, not definitive or positive. From a sceptical perspective, then, one must consider the possibility that the cat playing a game with a human may itself be wondering whether that human can think. This is because, for a sceptic, it is impossible to dismiss the possibility that a cat is thinking. Any attempt to refuse feline reasoning would be challenged with a question: how do you know? This question is unanswerable, and this unknowableness is at the heart of scepticism. For Sextus the inevitability of not knowing should lead the thinker to an abandonment of the search for truth. The sceptic finds philosophical tranquillity, he argues, in giving up the struggle to find answers.

The fact that such questions as "How do you know?" can be asked of philosophical truth-claims reminds us how fragile human reason is. And by extension we are also reminded how flimsy the arguments for human dominance are. For Montaigne, indeed, the relationship with pets exemplifies this. What is called pet "ownership" is actually rather different. It is collaborative, not a one-man show. As he wrote of his games with his cat, "If I have my time to begin or to refuse, so has she hers". This relationship with the cat is much more playful than the trained and apparently sober relation with the dog that sits at one's feet, but that does not mean that the philosophical tradition from which it emerges should be regarded as frivolous. Indeed, Montaigne's meditation has influenced the world that comes after it, and the scepticism that is contained in his question about his cat has re-emerged in recent years in the work of one of the most significant philosophers of the twentieth century. Pets once again are central to thinking.

In an essay entitled in its English translation "The Animal That Therefore I Am (More to Follow)", Jacques Derrida also contemplates his cat: a cat that, he insists, "isn't Montaigne's cat" (2002: 375) but his own *little cat* (*ibid*.: 374). This insistence marks, of course, Derrida's indebtedness to Montaigne even as it claims his independence from his predecessor. But Derrida's cat, unlike Montaigne's, is not involved in a game; rather, it is claiming its dues: "The cat follows me when I wake up, into the bathroom, asking for her breakfast, but she demands to be let out of that very room as soon as it (or she) sees me naked, ready for everything and resolved to make her wait" (*ibid*.: 382). It is this demand that Derrida is concerned with. For him, as for Montaigne, it opens up important philosophical questions and helps Derrida to position himself both alongside and at a distance from those philosophers who have never been, as he puts it, *seen seen* by the animal" (*ibid.*); that is, who have never acknowledged that the animal too is looking. "I often ask myself", Derrida writes: "just to see, *who I am* – and who I am (following) at the moment when, caught naked, in silence, by the gaze of an animal, for example the eyes of my cat, I have trouble, yes, a bad time overcoming my embarrassment" (*ibid.*: 372). The invocation here is of Aristotle's assertion in the *Rhetoric* that "no one feels shame before small children or animals" (II.6.1384b), an assertion that refuses to acknowledge the animal gaze and that is a foundation of the philosophy that Derrida is challenging. Aristotle's is a philosophy that denies subject status to animals because subject status is regarded as inseparable from the capacity for reason. Being a subject therefore is being human (and of course the stipulation that it is an *adult* human brings logical difficulties with it: at some point, it would seem, humans themselves are not really human at all). Derrida mounts his challenge against such an assumption of the link between human status and subject status in an utterly appropriate way: by speaking of a cat looking at him when he is naked. He turns from the concept of human shame towards an actual event in a bathroom: he moves from the abstract to the concrete.

Derrida thus repeats Montaigne's contemplation of his cat but does so in a particular way. Like Montaigne, he insists that this incident with his cat is a real encounter, "a scene", Derrida writes, "that is repeated every morning" (2002: 382). He describes the scene, returning insistently to his own nakedness, his *actual* nakedness. He speaks of the "impropriety that comes of finding oneself naked, one's sex exposed, stark naked before a cat that looks at you without moving, just to see" (*ibid.*: 373). He tells of his embarrassment at his embarrassment:

> Especially, I should make clear, if the cat observes me frontally naked, face to face, and if I am naked faced with the cat's eyes looking at me as it were from head to toe, just *to see*, not

> hesitating to concentrate its vision – in order to see, with a
> view to seeing – in the direction of my sex.   (*Ibid.*)

It is important to remember the power of Derrida's repeated return to his own nakedness *in a lecture*, in a medium in which he stands in front of an audience. The philosopher – the great mind – in fact asks his audience to view him as a body, and worse, as a *naked* body. In discussing his embarrassment at being embarrassed Derrida embarrasses himself.

But why this shameful behaviour? Why invite us, over and over again, to imagine his naked body? It is an attempt, I think, to undermine the arrogance that Derrida finds in the figure of the philosopher and in much philosophy. This is the arrogance that has separated mind from body, human from animal, and has been represented in the image of the philosopher with the dog at his feet. In this reading of the image the dog is a symbol of the power of human reason – that retriever of certainty – in that, just as the dog sits, obedient and subservient, at the philosopher's feet, so our bodies can be tamed and trained to submit to the domination of the mind. The dog in such philosophy is not really a dog at all; it is a symbol. For Montaigne and Derrida, however, the cat is real; there is an actual encounter that takes place in the world with another being and this reality is central to their thinking. To contemplate a dog as a mere abstraction (as "the Dog"), they seem to be arguing, is to reiterate the hierarchy that underpins humanist ideas. Instead they propose that we need to challenge this idea of contemplation's link to dominion. Derrida thus opens his discussion of animals in his bathroom, in this place that is so distant from the usual site of contemplation, the study. Derrida reminds us that the philosopher also has and is a body, and the concept of the philosopher as the great mind is undermined.

But there is more to Derrida's decision to locate his discussion in the bathroom. If a cat-flap provides a challenge to the boundary of the house, then the bathroom should be the last bastion of secure privacy in the home; it is perhaps the only room in the house to have a lock. But even here, Derrida argues, in our most private space, the cat poses a threat, and once again the concept of home as the site and source of human stability is challenged by a pet. This is a challenge Derrida is willing to take up: "The animal looks at us," he writes, "and we are naked before it. Thinking perhaps begins there" (2002: 397).

Derrida's thinking takes in many aspects of human–animal relations, but I want to mention just two. The first is his parenthesis when discussing his little cat: "(but a pussycat never belongs)" (*ibid*.: 376). The cat is Derrida's pet, but it is also, he acknowledges, a being in its own right. Placing this recognition in parentheses, however, represents Derrida's own difficulty in abandoning absolutely his own desire for possession and mastery; giving up one's status is hard. Thus, even while he asserts the cat's self-possession he calls it his own. Derrida can recognize the limitations of such thinking, but he cannot wholly abandon it. Such is the power of the philosophy he has inherited.

The second key point in the context of this discussion is Derrida's recognition of the use of animals as concepts in human thought. If we think about "the Dog" or "the Cat" we are not dealing with real animals but abstractions. We should, instead, be thinking about "this (individual) dog" or "that (particular) cat". Derrida argues that the concept "the Animal" – the general singular with a capital "A" – is a refusal to acknowledge difference, and is a, if not the, means by which the opposition human–animal is upheld. "Animal", he says, is a word "that men have given themselves at the origin of humanity and that they have given themselves in order to identify themselves, in order to recognize themselves, with a view to being what they say they are, namely men" (*ibid*.: 400).

A fracturing of the binary opposition of human and animal would thus undo the logic that persists in key conceptualizations of the human in Western philosophy. Aristotle's claims about human shame are premised on such an opposition, for example, as, of course, are the ideas of Descartes, a philosopher who found no reason to believe any animal had possession of an immortal soul because, as he wrote, "there is no reason to believe it of some animals without believing it of all, and many of them such as oysters and sponges are too imperfect for this to be credible" (1985: vol. III, 304). Derrida's refusal of the word "Animal" is a refusal of such logic. For him philosophy should recognize the vast difference not only between a dog and an oyster, but also between this cat and that one. Indeed, the title of Derrida's lecture signals Descartes as perhaps his key focus. In the original French the title is "L'Animal que donc je suis (à suivre)", which has been translated as "The Animal That Therefore I am (More to Follow)" by David Wills. This is obviously an invocation of Descartes's definition of the human mind, "je pense donc je suis" (I think therefore I am), and as such we can trace a complex philosophical journey (an "incredible journey", perhaps) in Derrida's essay from the dualism that separates human from animal, mind from body (traced in Aristotle's sense of shame), to doubt (Montaigne's game with his cat), back to dualism (Descartes's "I think therefore I am"), to doubt once again, when, in place of Descartes's formulation of the human of humanism, Derrida recognizes that his own humanity is never so fully present. *Je suis* – I am (here, now) – and *je suis* –I follow (there, after) – are the same in French and are placed alongside each other, or as simultaneous with each other. The self is thus understood to be present only as following: as being in movement rather than being, you might say, at home. Indeed, we can return to Montaigne once again to find a precursor of Derrida's assertion when the former writes, "We are never at home, we are always beyond" (2003: 9).

Pets, then – these individualized animals in the home – serve a vital philosophical function for the sceptic (and Derrida is certainly working within this tradition in his essay). They force us to remember that generalizations such as "the Animal" and statements based on such generalizations are meaningless. Thus, when Aristotle declares that "no one feels shame before small children or animals", a sceptical response (setting aside the issue of the status of children) should be: which animals? All of them, or just some? A dog *and* an oyster, or do you just mean an oyster? And if just the latter, why use the misleading generalization? Such questions may seem ridiculous, overly literal, but it is the literalness of the questions (like the reality of Derrida's encounter with his cat, and Montaigne's game with his) that is important. Derrida reminds us that philosophy must remember that humans and animals are real beings and not just abstract concepts. And as such, it is logical – for sceptics at least – that philosophy should think with pets, as they are the only real animals that many of us live with. Thinking about and with them transforms what it might be that thought is understood to be capable of.

But if the cat in its untrainability offers a vision that challenges human self-satisfaction does that mean that human–dog relations can never be recuperated for a philosophy that wishes to challenge human (and humanist) power? Is dog love always a veil for a relationship that rests on dominion? I want to turn to another way of thinking about human–dog relationships that opens up to view the limits of dog love. Donna Haraway's arguments propose that we can still live with dogs, but they offer very different concepts of "living with" from what has gone before. The humanists, it would seem, are not the only ones to think with dogs.

The training of the human

The orthodox "it" rather than "she or he" to refer to animals that I have used without comment so far in this book can be interpreted as in and of itself constructing animals in a particular way. Indeed, so grammatically orthodox is this object-making of the pet that even my word-processing system underlines "who" when used to refer to an animal, and offers the suggested replacement "that" instead. Likewise, the word "pet" constructs animals in a particular way; it does not simply label them. The word comes first of all from the eighteenth-century name for a hand-reared lamb, and evolves to become the term used to describe any non-working domestic animal that lives in the home. *The Oxford English Dictionary* proposes the definition: "An animal (typically one which is domestic or tame) kept for pleasure or companionship". But "pet", the *OED* notes, can also refer to "An indulged, spoiled, or favourite, child", and, as the verb "to pet" reveals, there is something demeaning in this choice of name for this group of animals. "Pet" can thus signal animals' infantilization, their inferior status, and calling an animal a pet could be regarded as reinforcing – without realizing that one is doing so, perhaps – the dominance that Yi-Fu Tuan recognized as central to all human–pet relations.

An alternative term for the animal "kept for pleasure" has emerged in recent years that is not simply a response to the directives of political correctness, that does not just re-label the bond. This new term recognizes something that exists in so many human–animal relationships that the word "pet" fails to account for. "Companion animal", the new term, emphasizes mutuality. Pets are no longer at our feet; they are by our side. And "companion animal" is not anthropomorphic: the label does not simply "upgrade" the animal to being *like* a human. It is a term that, it could be argued, refuses the possibility of anthropomorphism in that it states up front that some animals *are* (not *are like*, but actually *are*) our friends.

The American philosopher Donna Haraway also refuses some anthropomorphic representations of dogs but for a different reason, and in doing so recognizes the dangers of a conventional-ized concept of the pet. She has argued, for example, that:

contrary to lots of dangerous and unethical projection in the Western world that makes domestic canines into furry chil-dren, dogs are not about oneself. Indeed, that is the beauty of

dogs. They are not a projection, nor the realization of an intention, nor the telos of anything. They are dogs; i.e., a species in
obligatory, constitutive, historical, protean relationship with
human beings.   (2003: 11–12)

For Haraway, though, the concept of the "companion animal" is
too small, and she proposes instead what she regards as a "bigger
and more heterogeneous category": "companion species". Such
companion species include "rice, bees, tulips, and intestinal flora,
all of whom make life for humans what it is – and vice versa" (*ibid.*:
15). And that final phrase, "and vice versa", signals Haraway's most
significant step. Humans, she argues, are a companion species too:
"There cannot be just one companion species; there have to be at
least two to make one … none of the partners pre-exist the relating".
"If I have a dog, my dog has a human" (*ibid.*: 12). Mutuality finds its
place here not, as with Lassie, in the dog's decision to come home,
but in co-definition.

Thus for Haraway, embedded in the notion of the companion
species is a belief in the significance of relationships. She repeats
her point for emphasis: "Beings do not pre-exist their relatings"
(*ibid.*: 6). It thus makes sense when Haraway writes that "Dogs are
not surrogates for theory; they are not here just to think with. They
are here to live with" (*ibid.*: 5). If we do not pre-exist our relationships with dogs (and with all other companion species) how can we
merely think with them, she asks. A conception that allows animals
to be only ever symbolic, and for thinking to happen with such
symbolic creatures, presupposes the existence of humans prior to
animals (this echoes Heidegger's reading of anthropomorphism).
Rather, Haraway argues, it is by living with other companion species
– other real others – that we are enabled to be and thus to think.
Living comes before thinking.

So, like Montaigne and Derrida, Haraway refuses the symbolic
meaning of the animal, but unlike Montaigne and Derrida her

refusal is not in order to contemplate the nature of the human. Her *Companion Species Manifesto* (2003) was written in part to explore how "an ethics and politics committed to the flourishing of significant otherness [might] be learned from taking dog-human relationships seriously" (2003: 3). And one of the writers she turns to in order to do this is Vicki Hearne. If Stanley Coren believes that there is some place for doggerel in human–dog relations, Hearne, following her mentor William Koehler, despises such language; she writes of "the demeaning repertoire of so-called trainers who propose babbling at the dog as sweetly as possible" (2000: 45). But Hearne does not close off the possibility of human–canine communication: far from it. She outlines not only how to instigate a conversation with a dog, but how to make that conversation two-way, and what the moral implications of such a conversation might be. It is the inseparability of training, conversing and morality in Hearne's philosophy that is of interest to Haraway.

In a fascinating chapter entitled "How to Say 'Fetch'", Hearne discusses her dog-training methods and outlines how she trained the pointer bitch Salty. The training begins with basic – but not uncomplicated – commands ("Sit!" and its release, "Okay") and moves to teaching her to fetch. To do this Hearne places the fetch object, a dumbbell, in Salty's mouth and says "Fetch!" She then removes the dumbbell and praises the dog. This does not require Salty to do anything but allow Hearne to open her mouth and place the object in it. After a week or so, Salty has learnt to open her mouth when Hearne approaches with the dumbbell, and to wait obediently as Hearne says "Fetch!" Then, after a while, Hearne makes the dog reach forward to pick up the dumbbell herself on the command, with the threat of an ear-pinch if she does not do this. Eventually the dumbbell will be moved a few feet away, then further and further; and the dog will come to answer the command "Fetch!"

This sounds like a record of a successful training regime, but there is more to it than that. By training the dog Hearne argues that

she has higher aims: training, she writes, produces attentiveness –
of dog and of human – and the possibility of conversation, wit and
deception. These seem large claims for dog-training, but Hearne
argues how they can be made with great clarity. Having been the
silent partner in the training, one day, she writes:

> Salty gets my attention by sitting spontaneously in just the
> unmistakably symmetrical, clean-edged way of formal work.
> If I'm on the ball, if I respect her personhood at this point, I'll
> respond. Her sitting may have a number of meanings. "Please
> stop daydreaming and feed me!" ... Or it may mean, "Look, I
> can explain about the garbage can, it isn't the way it looks." In
> any case, if I respond, the flow of intention is now two-way,
> and the meaning of "Sit" has changed yet again. This time it is
> Salty who has enlarged the context.   (*Ibid.*: 56)

Derrida wondered what would happen if the animal responded,
and here we seem to have an answer. Salty and Hearne are having
a two-way, mutually meaningful conversation. And this conversation can include jokes:

> One day I absentmindedly fail to respond when Salty brings
> me her feed dish, a projection of "Fetch" she thought of. I
> put the dish on the desk and continue my work. Now she
> brings me a wastepaper basket, wriggling so hard with
> gleeful appreciation of her own wit she drops it on her way.
> ... There is a great deal to say about this, but all I want to say
> here is that I am struck by a new wonder at the priority of
> commands and also at how the coherence of the commands
> depends on my ability, my willingness, to hand authority
> over to Salty, in the case of the wastebasket by acknowl-
> edging the possibility of her saying something I haven't
> taught her to say.   (*Ibid.*: 75)

Hearne argues that, "Salty doesn't (can't) retrieve *for* me, she can only retrieve *with* me" (*ibid.*: 71). "Fetch" is a conversation, not a command, when both partners have learned to communicate. What might be termed the companionate activity of retrieving both requires and allows for this conversation (in Latin, *conversatus* means having lived with). This training, Hearne would argue, does not place the dog at the feet of the human at all.

Haraway recognizes in Hearne a fellow traveller: she too wants to claim mutuality in her conversations with her dogs, conversations that take the form of agility training. But there are differences between Hearne's and Haraway's conception of how the human–dog conversation can begin that are worth looking at. I mentioned above – deliberately briefly – that, as part of her training regime, Hearne used ear-pinching as a correction. Hearne, as Haraway notes, "remains a sharp thorn in the paw for the adherents of positive training methods" (2003: 48). Such adherents have moved away from the method Hearne used, which was first outlined by William Koehler, and which is, as Haraway puts it, "military-style ... [and] not so fondly remembered for corrections like leash jerks and ear pinches" (*ibid.*). Instead Haraway and others use the reward-giving and clicker-training method of "behaviorist learning theorists" (as advocated by Victoria Stilwell on Channel 4's *It's Me or the Dog*). This seems a vast difference of opinion about how dogs should be treated but, as Haraway's brief outline of Susan Garrett's positive training theory reveals, the difference may not be so great after all.

Haraway calls Garrett's behaviourist method "positive bondage" (*ibid.*: 43). Rewarding the dog with liver treats may seem liberal, Haraway writes, but this is anything but the truth: "positive does not mean permissive. Indeed, I have never read a dog-training manual more committed to near total control in the interests of fulfilling human intentions, in this case, peak performance in a demanding, dual species, competitive sport" (*ibid.*: 43–4). While Garrett uses rewards and Hearne uses physical correction, they are, as Haraway notes, "blood sisters under the skin" (*ibid.*: 48). At the beginning of their conversations – at the moment when the relationship with the dog is instigated – both Garrett and Hearne recognize the importance of the commanding human and the obedient dog. Teaching a dog to sit is, after all, placing it at one's feet whether one achieves this with pinches or treats (although I know which I would prefer). But Haraway would argue, I think, that this training of dogs has very different implications to that represented in medieval and Renaissance iconography; you might say that both training methods – Hearne's and Garrett's – begin with dominion *in order to uproot it*. On the one hand, Hearne argues that training "ennobles" the dog, but on the other she is much more practical:

> It won't do to suggest that the dog can just live peacefully around the house while we refrain from giving any commands that might deprive him of his "freedom," for that simply doesn't happen. We are in charge already, like it or not. ... One might as well suggest that we leave off keeping toddlers out of the street or teaching anyone anything at all. We do assume authority over each other constantly. ... A refusal to give commands or to notice that commands are being given is often a refusal to acknowledge a relationship, just as is a refusal to obey. (2000: 48–9)

Hearne, following the ideas of Friedrich Nietzsche, sees a will to power at the heart of all (human–human, as well as human–animal, and animal–animal) relationships, and argues that rights emerge through successful interactions. "We don't imagine we can grant civil rights to human beings", she writes, "without first assuming authority over them as teachers, parents and friends" (*ibid.*: 49). And we should imagine the same to be true of animals. It is not the fact that it is an animal that should give a dog rights (no one would wish to grant rights, Hearne would argue, to a dangerous dog). Rights are granted because the animal can be trusted, and trust is a product of training; it is the product of a relationship:

> Salty's right to the freedom of the house … like my right to the freedom of the house, is contingent on making a limited number and kind of messes, respecting other people's privacy, refraining from leaping uninvited onto furniture and laps and making the right distinctions between mine and thine, especially in the matter of food dishes. (*Ibid.*: 53)

Indeed, it is this trust that the rules will be obeyed (by human and dog) that allows for the dog's sense of humour to be made evident: "I now trust Salty enough so that although the general rule is no-dogs-on-the-furniture, I know that if she should once in a blue moon get up on my chair, she is making some sort of joke" (*ibid.*: 75). Without the rules and the training, Hearne argues, there could be no access to this canine humour; without ear-pinching there would be no dog jokes; and thus without hierarchy there would be no conversation.

There thus appears to be a paradox. Salty sits on the chair only because she knows that she should be on the floor at her human's feet, but Hearne proposes that training is more than the re-enactment of dominion. She argues that it produces a dog of nobility and wit, it allows for a conversation (which can be led by the dog as well as the human), and transforms the status of both dog and human, and it is this latter point – which is echoed in Haraway's recognition that humans are a companion species too – that is most important. Hearne becomes attentive to Salty, Salty becomes attentive to Hearne and both become something else in the relationship.

Without using the notion of rights as Hearne does, Haraway recognizes something similar. Writing to the trainer she and her dog work with, she acknowledges the equality of human and canine in the training when she names them "Your pupils, Roland Dog and I" (2003: 57). It is in the relationship that both are made. Thus the transformation of Roland Dog and Donna Human comes from each learning to pay proper attention to the other. Haraway writes:

> In short, the major demand on the human is precisely what most of us don't even know we don't know how to do – to wit, how to see who the dogs are and hear what they are telling us, not in bloodless abstraction, but in one-on-one relationship, in otherness-in-connection. (*Ibid*.: 45)

It is not in "bloodless abstraction" – not in thinking about that abstraction "the Dog" – that this can happen, but through real companionship. And it is such attentive interrelations that lead to a development of respect and responsibility, she argues, which is also known as love.

Haraway dismisses one of the ways in which dogs are anthropomorphized. She states, "I resist being called the 'mom' to my dogs because I fear infantilization of the adult canines and misidentification of the important fact that I wanted dogs, not babies" (*ibid*.: 95–6). But she applauds Hearne's use of anthropomorphic language in her description of dogs' responses. The anthropomorphism Hearne uses (stressing the dogs' intention, their capacity for understanding) is valuable, Haraway argues, in order "to keep the humans alert to the fact that somebody is at home in the animals they work with". And she continues:

> Just *who* is at home must permanently be in question. The recognition that one cannot *know* the other or the self, but must ask in respect for all of time who and what are emerging in relationship, is the key. That is so for all true lovers, of whatever species. (*Ibid*.: 50)

This "negative way of knowing" as she terms it, uses the tools of scepticism but moves away from unknowing to construct a new ethical framework based not on status in individuality (Descartes's representation of the thinking human subject) but on the status of and in what she terms significant otherness: "I believe that all ethical relating, within or between species, is knit from the silk-strong thread of ongoing alertness to otherness-in-relation. We are not one, and being depends on getting on together" (*ibid.*).

Haraway's ethical stance here is not absolute but situated: that is, ethical relations happen at specific times and in specific places, between this being and that being. Ethics are not abstract (like, for example, the claim that "no one feels shame before small children or animals") but are particular. Haraway also argues that there is a "bestiary of agencies" that construct the world: not just human agency (*ibid.*: 6). Animals (and rice and bees, and tulips and intestinal flora), like humans, make the world they live in, but all beings make in different ways. Agility training is Haraway's vision of how these "non-harmonious agencies" (*ibid.*: 7) might work in harmony:

> the task is to become coherent enough in an incoherent world to engage in a joint dance of being that breeds respect and response in the flesh, in the run, on the course. And then to remember how to live like that at every scale, with all part-ners.   (*Ibid.*: 62)

"And then": this is a crucial linking clause. The agility training is, she argues, never a symbol. Haraway uses her sportswriter father as her exemplar for her own writing method. She is, she notes, doing what he did when he wrote up a game of baseball for a newspaper: "spinning a story that is just the facts". Agility training here really is agility training (just as baseball really was baseball for her father, and just as cats really were cats for Montaigne and Derrida). But the interaction between dog and human that the training requires and produces stands also as a model for other kinds of interaction. Successful completion of the course requires successful cohabitation, whatever the activity. We live and find our being in relationships; we are all companion species.

Thus for Haraway, it is possible to have a human–dog relationship that does not simply replicate the image of the dog at the feet of the human, and does not simply repeat the myth of the dog coming home. But to achieve this relationship Haraway and her mentors, Garrett and Hearne, recognize the need for training, and all claim in this training the possibility of enhancing the life of the dog as well as the human. This is, perhaps, an uncomfortable truth about living with a pet: it will always require an exercise of what might be called dominion even if the ultimate aim is cohabitation rather than coercion (Hearne argues that this is true of all human–human relationships too). As Haraway reveals, all training – using Koehler's or Garrett's method – is initially at least about the fulfilment of human intentions; the animal is always, at first, being constructed for and by the human. Thus, living with a dog will always transform the dog. But, she argues, *it will also transform the human*, and this is central to Haraway's work. For her there is a sense of the human, like the animal, as unmade before its relations with its many and varied companion species (how could we live without our intestinal fauna?). Living in the world is constructing the self from the relationships in and with that world: we do not pre-exist our relatings. For Haraway, recognizing this should breed respect for that world.

This might seem to be a final step for dog owners (cat owners must inhabit their relationship with their companion in other ways). The aim of a truly mutual human–dog relationship in the home is not of the silent animal sitting at one's feet, but of a conversation that can be led by the human or the canine member of the partnership. But an acknowledgement that training is necessary for such successful cohabitation is also an acknowledgement that having a companion that is an animal is always a relationship that at least begins with the human in charge even if it doesn't end there. To say this, of course, could be to say that human–pet relations – and human–companion animal relations, and all companion species relations between humans and animals in the home – are always hierarchical at heart. And such a recognition does bring with it melancholic anxiety that the conversations – even if happy, even if two-way – are somehow in the final instance produced by human dominance. A final achievement, it would seem, might be to engage with an animal in a way that did not dictate even that level of control, and it is to such a possibility and its implications that I now turn.

The rebuilding of the home

"As a member of the House Rabbit Society (HRS) who has rescued 200 rabbits and lived with them in my house, I want to live with rabbits as companion animals … But I also worry that this entails considerable subjugation" (Smith 2003: 181). So begins literary scholar Julie Ann Smith's discussion "Beyond Dominance and Affection: Living with Rabbits in Post-Humanist Households". Immediately, in the title of her discussion, we can see how Smith distances herself from some issues that have been discussed so far in this book. Yi-Fu Tuan's thesis is left behind; she wants to go beyond his sense of dominance as being simply veiled by affection in human–pet relations. Here animals are "companion animals" rather than pets and the threat of the infantilization of the animals is removed. But as well as leaving these existing ideas behind, Smith offers a new one: here the human is *post*-human, a concept I shall return to.

Smith's discussion of living with rabbits takes us back to our starting-point, the human home, and is fascinating in its challenge to many of the assumptions that we have about ourselves and how we live in the modern world. She writes that "members [of the HRS] surrendered enormous control over their homes":

> Many ... "rabbit proofed" their houses, a playful word that euphemized extensive modifications. In my own house, rabbit-proofing meant that most of the furniture was made of metal, electrical cords were fastened behind furniture or covered in hard plastic or metal tubing, and protective wood strips were tacked on to wood baseboards and wood trim around closets and windows. In addition, linoleum replaced carpet – or the carpet was abandoned to shredding – and fencing enclosed bookcases.   (2003: 187)

Such dedication to making the home a space for both its human and its animal inhabitants is in many ways shocking, but is also logical, and this is surely where the real shock resides. "[A]s more humans feel free to insist on the 'humanity' of their companion animals", Smith writes, "they feel more tension between the presumption of equality and the ways they actually live with animals" (*ibid*.: 183). There are two possible solutions to this tension that exists at the heart of all human–pet (or human–companion animal) relations. The first is that we refuse to contemplate the "humanity" of the animal and thus live with it as a lesser being. The outcome of this, however, is that we can no longer tell ourselves the story of such an animal's love, as love relies on just the kind of subjectivity that has been refused. The second possible solution to the "tension between the presumption of equality and the ways [people] actually live with animals" is the one Smith's proposes: it is to accept the logic of humanization that sits at the heart of the relationship but without accepting the anthropocentrism of such an idea. What Smith proposes is that we acknowledge the animal in the home as a full member of the household and so transform the home to fit the animal; if child-proofing is regarded as a parental duty, rabbit-proofing should be seen as a companionate one.

This transformation produces not only a new home but also a new ethical framework, and a new sense of the human. Despite the analogy between child-proofing and rabbit-proofing, the disappearance of the paternalism of pet ownership, in which the human stands as parent to the infantilized animal, is gone in Smith's model. In its place is what she terms "performance ethics". By this she means something similar to Haraway's belief in a situated ethics. Smith proposes that a key part of performance ethics is an "attentive provision of opportunities for animal agency and recognition that animals actively utilize these to perform their own natures" (2003: 182). "In other words, 'performance' corrects the idea of animals as a blank materiality that needs the human mind to be meaningful" (*ibid*.: 192): it acknowledges and allows for the fact that there is something that it is like to be a companion animal.

For Smith, then, ethics between humans and companion animals is two-way: both parties are actors, both parties can lead the conversation. Thus, for example, any training that takes place is not really training at all: "So-called 'litterbox training'", she writes, "primarily meant capitalizing on the rabbit habit of urinating consistently in one or two places. We simply put litterboxes where the rabbits decided to eliminate" (*ibid*.: 187). Likewise Smith records how animal agency is central to human interior design to the extent that she writes of "Rabbit ideas of space management" that dictate the organization of the home:

> Over time, we came to understand the principles of rabbit space and changed our abodes even more. After many years of living with rabbits, I noticed that they liked free corridors along perimeters. Before this, I would dutifully place litterboxes and toys along the walls of the playroom after I had cleaned each day. By night, the room was a "mess". Eventually I noticed that

it was a particular kind of mess: Everything moveable in the room was in the middle of the floor. This observation changed forever the way I live in my house.   (*Ibid.*: 188)

The conversation takes a long time to get underway. Smith lived with the rabbits for "many years" before she understood what they were saying. But understanding does come into being; "mess" is reconfigured as meaningful communication. Smith learns to read the rabbits and to respond to their responses. Smith, you might say, is trained by the rabbits.

Smith also recognizes "other rabbit preferences". They prefer, she realizes, "spaces that allow them to see out but not to be seen" (*ibid.*: 189). What is being acknowledged here is the agency of the rabbits – the fact that they are seeing – and, because this is acknowledged, Smith reorganizes her home to encourage that agency to be exercised. It is no surprise (either philosophically or domestically) therefore that this new conception of the animal should lead to a reconceptualization of both human and rabbit identity. The home and our humanity are turned over to the rabbits, and human dominion is given up. Different from the humanist stories of pet ownership, in this story, these rabbits do not return home and bring with them our humanity, but nor do they undergo the kind of training that Haraway outlines in order to become companions (Smith recognizes that dogs have different requirements from rabbits). The kind of companion that the rabbits are has changed and this changes the kind of companion that Smith is.

In another essay, in which she discusses the rabbits' perception of death (something that humanist philosophy denies that animals possess – a denial that Smith challenges) Smith recalls an experiment she undertook with one of the rabbits:

Rose often sat next to me while I worked at the computer, and I would bend over to stroke her ears. One day I decided to test Rose to see which part of my body she thought of as "me." For the first time in her presence, I laid myself out on the floor. I thought she would sit by me somewhere. I hoped that she would sit by my head, proving that she knew where "I" really was. As all rabbits will, Rose took the configuration of this new impediment on the floor, mapping out my body in relation to the furniture and passages of escape. She then identified one of my hands and started biting me. What was important to her was the pleasure of our interactions, and she adeptly found the instrument of our relationship and implemented a strategy for activating it. (2005: 199)

It is when Smith changes the relationship from being one in which (once again) the human has the animal at her feet (although Smith is already bending over) that a new sense of human and animal self emerges. Smith, lying on the floor alongside the rabbit, is disappointed that Rose does not sit by her head to engage with her. Smith self-consciously reflects on how far she holds on to a humanist concept of subjectivity that places human selfhood in the place of thinking – the brain – just, perhaps, as Derrida cannot quite give up the idea that his little cat is *his* little cat. But Smith recognizes that the rabbit's choice of her hand as the important site of the relationship is logical: it is the hand that touches the rabbit, that is the source of pleasure. But it is also more than just logical; Rose's focus on Smith's hand reminds us that to a companion animal we are not the beings we might think we are, because companion animals – of whatever species – make sense of us from their own perspective, read us through their own senses, and thus potentially experience something of us that we do not. The same, we can assume, is true of our experience of animals: what we think they are is not what they think they are.

But if, for Rose, the site of Smith's identity – her self – is her hand, this is not an error. It merely reminds us – as Derrida did

– that we are mind and body, head and hand. And this reinterpretation of the self works for both partners in the relationship. As Rose reads Smith's body differently from the way Smith herself does, so Smith is aware that she reads the rabbits differently from the rabbits themselves. Rabbit physiology, like human physiology, has a role to play in this discussion:

> rabbits do not lend themselves to easy interpretation. Rather, they frustrate intellectual mastery, destabilize human confidence in the ability to speak authoritatively about them. We recognize that their bodies – for example, their ways of seeing – put limits on our abilities to know them. (2005: 194)

Because rabbits' eyes are "placed high and to the sides of the skull" it can appear that rabbits do not look back when we look at them. Smith writes of "a mutual" gaze with the rabbit, That "The rabbit also looked at me, but because of his kind of vision, he seemed less aware of me, less able to know me as a 'self'" (*ibid.*: 194). This is because the rabbit's eyes are placed differently to the human's. Smith writes: "unless I studiously reorient my view" of rabbits, they can seem distant as their gaze seems to be directed away from what they actually see, and their appearance "can thus encourage a sense of humans being more aware and more 'real' than they are" (*ibid.*: 195).

The recognition that an animal can return our gaze – which Derrida also acknowledged in his bathroom – challenges the humanist belief that only humans have the capacity to participate in such acts of acknowledgement of and engagement with other beings. But rabbit physiology in many ways appears to aid the humanist construction of animals, not only because rabbits do not look like us, but because rabbits do not look the way we look. Acknowledging that her own human body is seen differently by Rose than the way Smith herself sees it reminds us that the relationship

– and its difficulties – work both ways. Like Montaigne, who knew of his game with his cat that, "If I have my time to begin or to refuse, so has she hers", so Smith knows that she is as other to the rabbit as the rabbit is to her, and that it is from this perspective that the relationship is formed. Trying to see the rabbit in another way – trying to look beyond the rabbit's failure to be human and see the rabbit as a rabbit – is difficult but necessary. It is difficult because it works against all the ideas that are so central to our concept of human selfhood, and these, of course, include how we perceive animals. To accept that an animal can look at us, just as we can look at an animal, you might say, is not only to acknowledge, as Derrida did, that we are being "seen seen", it is also to accept that animals are not just objects for us to look upon, but are subjects like us. (In these terms zoos become morally very problematic places.)

This, I think, is where Smith's concept of the post-human comes in. She writes of the activities of HRS members that "Many of us found it easier to change ourselves than the premises" (2003: 187). She is writing about the home here, but the premises she refers to could also be philosophical premises: the foundations of thought. The logic of the humanization of the pet – the fact that it is an animal in the home, that it is family rather than food, that it is inside not outside – can only be fully articulated, Smith is arguing, if humans change their view of themselves. The transformation of the home is simply to be understood as an externalized alteration. The more important change takes place within, and, for Smith, the human must become a post-human.

The prefix "post-" here could simply signify chronology: thus the post-human is a conception of the human that comes after humanism. Such a reading is both true and false: true because post-humanist ideas certainly require humanist ones to be in place; but false because the emergence of a thing called the post-human does not signal the end of humanism – we are not *after humanism* with the post-human. Far from it: the shock-value of Smith's discussion of the way she has transformed her home lies in the continued and orthodox belief that the pet should be at our feet; that we should not be lying on the floor alongside our companion animals. It works because she knows that we know what humanism is to the extent that it is like the air we breathe when we think about living with animals.

But post-humanism can have another meaning, a meaning that is formulated around an undoing of the humanist construction of the human. Post-humanist philosophy rejects the humanist human, that being that exists in isolation and that is sought in the mind, and celebrates something else: something that is more playful, more collaborative, more infiltrated by its others. It is possible to see, I hope, that Smith's announcement that she lives in a post-humanist household follows such a reading of the term. She recognizes herself as both head and hand, as mind and body, human and animal. And in this recognition of her ambiguous status, she asserts her capacity to live with the rabbits.

We should not forget that it is with rabbits that Smith is able to have this domestic relationship. It would not be possible, as Hearne, Thomas and Smith know, to live with dogs without any kind of training or containment (and Smith does note the ethical problem inherent in her decision to spay the rabbits she lives with). But, whatever its limitations, Smith's record of her life with rabbits offers us a glimpse of another possibility. If Lassie lying by the Carraclough's fire is one image of ideal human–animal domestic relations, then Julie Ann Smith lying by her desk might be another. But perhaps, as Derrida and Haraway have shown us, there is a happy medium: there are simultaneously locked doors and cat flaps; there is at the same time training and talking in our relations with our pets.

5. Conclusion

This is not simply a narrative of progress. Thinking is changing but things have not just got better. There have been massive shifts in the ways in which we live: the industrial revolution, urbanization, globalization – all have had and are having their impact on the lives of humans and animals. Being a pet now is not the same as being a pet in 1800. There have been very important changes in consumer culture, health care, legal status and so on that seem to emphasize the increasingly equal status of these animals. But attitudes have also persisted across time that reveal the position of the animal in the home to be ambiguous in other ways. Indeed, there is one paradox that I want to explore here. I want to propose that one way of thinking about being equal – of claiming a pet's human-like status – may be a reason for one of the clearest displays of what philosopher Clare Palmer has called "an attitude of instrumentalism" (2006: 182). This, she writes, is present in human–pet relations in a way that is "unsettling in a relationship described … in terms of companionship or the familial" (*ibid.*). It is by making our pets human-like that we also, it seems, make them into objects.

Novelist J. M. Coetzee offers one glimpse of this paradox. In his novel *Disgrace*, which was published in 1999, the same year as *King* and *Timbuktu*, and which also deals in themes of home, loss and human–dog relations, the problem is presented very simply by the central character, who is doing voluntary work helping to euthanize dogs in an animal clinic. "The dogs are brought to the clinic because they are unwanted: *because we are too menny*" (1999a: 146). The phrase Coetzee places in italics, as literary critic Philip Armstrong notes, is a quotation from Thomas Hardy's novel *Jude the Obscure*, and comes "from the note left by Jude's eldest child when he hangs himself and his siblings, believing this sacrifice will free his parents from the increasingly difficult task of providing for them" (2008: 180). But of course "*too menny*" does not simply represent over-abundance. It places humans and animals on the same level, not to illustrate the animalization of humans but to think about the full implications of pet-hood in the modern world.

"*Too menny*" is a pun that plays on an issue that sits at the heart of human–pet relations. Humans have produced vast numbers of animals that are of a different kind to non-domesticated ones. They are both human and animal (Leach's "man-animals") and are often just too menny, too human-like to live without humans (they might survive, but packs of feral dogs are perceived as dangerous and thus cannot be allowed to live). And yet, despite the fact that we humans are implicated in the evolution and production of pets, we don't want them all. What might appear to be an emotional relationship premised on the individuality of the animal is revealed in fact to be founded on and inseparable from ideas that objectify it (and here "it" is the appropriate pronoun). To say that pets are "*too menny*" is to acknowledge two things simultaneously: humanization and disposability.

Palmer cites some shocking statistics: "it is estimated that between 6 and 10 million dogs and between 7 and 10 million cats were humanely killed in pet shelters in the United States in 1990. This is somewhere between one-tenth and one-quarter of the total US dog and cat population" (Palmer 2006: 170–71). She notes too the appalling calculation that Tuan records: that, on average, "households keep their pets for only two years" (Tuan 1984: 8, cited in Palmer 2006: 171). Palmer writes, with a degree of understate-ment, that the "concept of pet-keeping as the benign guardianship of companion animals sits uneasily" with such figures (2006: 170).

How can we simultaneously claim pets as our kin and regard them "as expendable individuals that can be killed en masse at human will – or even whim" (ibid.: 171)? If Smith pointed out one paradox in our simultaneous anthropomorphism of our pets and our treatment of them as less than human, the paradox that Palmer highlights is perhaps even more problematic. How can we so easily kill the things we apparently love?

Of course, many pet owners do not abandon healthy pets, and many animals are allowed to live out their natural lives with their human companions. But the statistics do not lie. There are too many pets, whether because of unwanted litters or because the pet industry produces abundance in response to perceived customer demand (Erica Sheen [2005] discusses the possible over-breeding of Dalmatians in advance of the release of Disney's live action *101 Dalmatians* in 1994, for example). Not all of the animals that are available to be pets will find permanent homes, and some of those that do will find that those homes, for a variety of reasons, are not permanent after all. Animal shelters re-home where they can, but there will always be a discrepancy between the number of animals available and the number that are rescued. Those animals that fail to get homed or re-homed are often humanely killed ("humane", of course, being an interesting word in this context). This, it would seem, is the normal state of affairs in the world of pets. If the highest statistic that Palmer cites is right, then a rate of overabundance (perhaps I should stop euphemizing and call it overproduction) of 25 per cent is possible: for every four healthy companion animals one is destined to be killed unnecessarily.

What is the way forward? Neutering is one possibility advocated by numerous animal welfare organizations. But the thinkers I have been looking at here offer other ways of addressing the issue. Donna Haraway's notion of inter-reliance – of our existence only as a companion species – opens up a new way of thinking about our relationships with pets. Here we recognize ourselves, our humanity, as embedded in networks that can include our animal companions in a way that reminds us of our essential indebtedness to them. In such a framework the destruction of healthy animals becomes a different kind of problem, and one that rebounds on our notion of what it means to be not so much humane as human. Smith's reconstruction of her home is another response to the paradoxes that persist in pet ownership. For her, living with rescued animals on terms that allow for the agency of those animals to be exercised is the ideal that, once again, requires a re-assessment of what it means to be a human. This, of course, transforms human–pet relationships into something else: something so different from what we now hold to be conventional as to challenge many of our ways of understanding our selves and our world. For this reason, for its very challenge to how we think, Smith's solution seems impossible (and "seems", of course, does not mean "is").

But, perhaps more than anything what pets remind us of is that it is not only animals that need to be trained to co-habit. Living as a human requires careful training; it is premised on the monitoring of boundaries, and needs us to be involved in compassionate contemplation, all of which pets provide opportunities for. But living as a human is also enhanced by and reliant on imaginative thinking, and pets again offer occasion for this. In such contexts, where pets help us to construct who we are, where we are reminded of our embeddedness in relationships, the killing of healthy animals that are surplus to requirement might tell us much about what it currently means to be human. Whether we can become better – perhaps *less menny* – people through living with and thinking with pets is up to us.

Further reading

There are, as any quick look at the shelves in most bookshops will show, many, many books on pets available. Some are memoirs, some psychological accounts, some training manuals, some all three. And philosophical speculation has its place here. So, where to begin reading? Anyone interested in exploring things further should read Elizabeth Marshall Thomas's *The Hidden Lives of Dogs* (2003), a study that attempts to look inside dog lives and voices a fascination with the non-humans with whom we share a home. It is a text that has influenced many subsequent writers. *Dogs Never Lie About Love* (1997) brings together Jeffrey Moussaieff Masson's work as a psychoanalyst and his love for and fascination with his three dogs. What he proposes is an emotional encounter between humans and animals in the domestic space of the home. And Stanley Coren's *How to Speak Dog* (2001) is at once a practical manual and an account of the behaviour and capacity of the dog touching on issues of language and understanding that are central to any encounter with animals. Questions of animal minds are the focus of Marian Stamp Dawkins's *Through Our Eyes Only?* (1993) and Lesley J. Rogers's *Minds of Their Own* (1997).

Perhaps the most influential scholarly argument to be presented about human relationships with pets – and one that has a central presence in my own thinking – is Yi-Fu Tuan's *Dominance and Affection* (1984). I would advise anyone interested in exploring human–pet relations to look at his uncomfortable thesis about power and control. But from a very different perspective, Marjorie Garber's *Dog Love* (1997) is a great survey and celebration of all things dog in contemporary culture, touching as it does on films, literature, dog shows and more. Donna Haraway's most recent study *When Species Meet* (2008) expands the argument of *The Companion Species Manifesto* (2003), which I explore in Chapter 4, and offers a fascinating perspective on the worlds of dogs, breeding, commerce and love. Further writings on animals by Jacques Derrida have recently been translated into English and are available in *The Animal That Therefore I Am* (2008).

Historical accounts of pet ownership offer another perspective on some of the discussions in my own work as well as a longer view of humans' relationships with their non-human kin. Kathleen Kete's wonderful and surprising exploration of nineteenth-century Parisian petkeeping and its cultural meanings in *The Beast in the Boudoir* (1994) is an excellent starting-point. In it she looks at a range of issues being raised by the emergence of modern pet ownership: welfare, loyalty, fear of rabies. Harriet Ritvo's analysis of the surfacing of nationalism in nineteenth-century dog breeding and dog shows in *The Animal Estate* (1990) has become a classic account, as has James Serpell's *In the Company of Animals* (1986), which takes a transcultural as well as historical perspective on human–pet relations.

The field of what is called animal studies in the humanities is a fast expanding one that looks at the role of non-humans in history, culture and society. Many important books from this field have helped me and are referred to in the bibliography, but a useful introduction to some of the debates, and to some cultural and philosophical questions about animals in general being raised by scholars working in this field is my own book *Animal* (2002).

Bibliography

Alger, J. M. & S. F. Alger 1999. "Cat Culture, Human Culture: An Ethnographic Study of a Cat Shelter". *Society & Animals* **7**(3): 199–218.

Aristotle 1952. *The Works of Aristotle*, W. Rhys Roberts (trans.). Chicago, IL: Encyclopaedia Britannica.

Armstrong, P. 2008. *What Animals Mean in the Fiction of Modernity*. London: Routledge.

Atkinson, E. [1912] 1994. *Greyfriar's Bobby*. Harmondsworth: Puffin.

Auster, P. 1999. *Timbuktu*. London: Faber.

Bauman, Z. 1998. *Globalization: The Human Consequences*. Cambridge: Polity.

Berger, J. 1980. "Why Look at Animals?". In his *About Looking*, 1–26. London: Writers & Readers Publishing Cooperative.

Berger, J. 1991. *And Our Faces, My Heart, Brief as Photos*. New York: Vintage.

Berger, J. 1999. *King: A Street Story*. London: Bloomsbury.

Bodson, L. 2000. "Motivation for Pet-Keeping in Ancient Greece and Rome". In *Companion Animals and Us*, A. L. Podberscek, E. S. Paul & J. A. Serpell (eds), 27–41. Cambridge: Cambridge University Press.

Burnford, S. 1960. *The Incredible Journey*. London: Hodder & Stoughton.

Cixous, H. 2006. "The Cat's Arrival". *Parallax* **12**(1): 21–42.

Coetzee, J. M. 1999a. *Disgrace*. London: Vintage.

Coetzee, J. M. 1999b. *The Lives of Animals*, A. Gutmann (ed.). Princeton, NJ: Princeton University Press.

Coren, S. 2001. *How to Speak Dog*. New York: Fireside.

Cottingham, J. 1978. "A 'Brute To Brutes'?: Descartes' Treatment of Animals". *Philosophy* **53**: 551–9.

Coupe, L. 1997. *Myth*. London: Routledge.

Davies, T. 1997. *Humanism*. London: Routledge.

Dawkins, M. S. 1998. *Through our Eyes Only? The Search for Animal Consciousness*. Oxford: Oxford University Pres.

Derrida, J. 2002. "The Animal that Therefore I Am (More to Follow)", D. Wills (trans.). *Critical Inquiry* **28**: 369–417.

Derrida, J. 2003. "And Say the Animal Responded?". In *Zoonologies: The Question of the Animal*, C. Wolfe (ed.), 121–46. Minneapolis, MN: University of Minnesota Press.

Derrida, J. 2008. *The Animal That Therefore I Am*. New York: Fordham University Press.

Descartes, R. 1985. *The Philosophical Writings of René Descartes*, J. Cottingham, R. Stoothoff & D. Murdoch (eds), 3 vols. Cambridge: Cambridge University Press.

Donald, D. 2008. *Picturing Animals in Britain*. New Haven, CT: Yale University Press.

Douglas, M. 1991. "The Idea of A Home: A Kind of Space". *Social Research* **58**(1): 287–307.

Douglas, M. 2006. *Purity and Danger: An Analysis of the Concept of Pollution and Taboo*. London: Routledge.

Eagleton, T. 1983. *Literary Theory: An Introduction*. Oxford: Blackwell.

Franklin, A. 1999. *Animals and Modern Cultures: A Sociology of Human–Animal Relations in Modernity*. London: Sage.

Fudge, E. 2002. *Animal*. London: Reaktion.

Garber, M. 1997. *Dog Love*. London: Hamish Hamilton.

Greenebaum, J. 2004. "It's a Dog's Life: Elevating from Pet to 'Fur Baby' at Yappy Hour". *Society & Animals* **12**(2): 117–35. www.animalsandsociety.org/assets/library/532_s1222.pdf (accessed July 2008).

Grier, K. C. 2006. *Pets in America: A History*. Chapel Hill, NC: University of North Carolina Press.

Haraway, D. 2003. *Companion Species Manifesto*. Chicago, IL: Prickly Paradigm Press.

Haraway, D. 2008. *When Species Meet*. Minneapolis, MN: University of Minnesota Press.

Hearne, V. 2000. *Adam's Task: Calling Animals by Name*. Pleasantville: Akadine Press.

Kete, K. 1994. *The Beast in the Boudoir: Petkeeping in Nineteenth-Century Paris*. Berkeley, CA: University of California Press.

Knight, E. 1981. *Lassie Come-Home*. Harmondsworth: Penguin.

Knight, E. [1938] 1990. "Lassie Come-Home". In *Dog Tales*, M. Beck (ed.), 25–48. London: Viking.

Kuzniar, A. A. 2006. *Melancholia's Dog: Reflections on our Animal Kinship*. Chicago, IL: University of Chicago Press.

Leach, E. 1966. "Anthropological Aspects of Language: Animal Categories and Verbal Abuse". In *New Directions in the Study of Language*, E. H. Lenneberg (ed.), 23–63. Cambridge, MA: MIT Press.

Masson, J. M. 1997. *Dogs Never Lie About Love*. New York: Random House.

McHugh, S. 2004. *Dog*. London: Reaktion.

Montaigne, M. de, 2003. "Our Feelings Reach out Beyond Us". In *The Complete Works*, D. M. Frame (trans.), 9–16. London: Everyman.

Montaigne, M. de 2003. "Apology for Raymond Sebond". In *The Complete Works*, D. M. Frame (trans.), 386–556. London: Everyman.

Nagel, T. 1974. "What is it Like to be a Bat?". *Philosophical Review* **83**(4): 435–51.

Palmer, C. 2006. "Killing Animals in Animal Shelters". In *Killing Animals*, The Animal Studies Group (ed.), 170–87. Champaign, IL: University of Illinois Press.

Peters, J. D. 1999. "Exile, Nomadism, and Diaspora: The Stakes of Mobility in the Western Canon". In *Home, Exile, Homeland: Film, Media, and the Politics of Place*, H. Naficy (ed.), 17–41. London: Routledge.

Puttenham, G. [1589] 1970. *The Arte of English Poesie*. Kent, OH: Kent State University Press.

Reutersward, P. 1991. "The Dog in the Humanist's Study". In *The Visible and Invisible in Art: Essays in the History of Art*, 206–25. Vienna: IRSA.

Ritvo, H. 1990. *The Animal Estate: The English and Other Creatures in the Victorian Age*. Harmondsworth: Penguin.

Rhodes, D. 2004. *Timoleon Vieta Come Home*. Edinburgh: Canongate.

Rogers, L. J. 1997. *Minds of Their Own: Thinking and Awareness in Animals*. London: Allen & Unwin.

Rushdie, S. 2006. *Midnight's Children*. London: Vintage.

Ryder, R. 1983. *Victims of Science: The Use of Animals in Research*, rev. edn. London: National Anti-Vivisection Society.

Saunders, M. M. 1965. *Beautiful Joe*. New York: Golden Press.

Serpell, J. 1986. *In the Company of Animals*. Oxford: Blackwell.

Serpell, J. 2003. "Anthropomorphism and Anthropomorphic Selection: Beyond the 'Cute Response'". *Society & Animals* **11**(1): 83–100.

Sextus Empiricus 2000. *The Outlines of Scepticism*, J. Annas & J. Barnes (eds). Cambridge: Cambridge University Press.

Sheen, E. 2005. "101 and Counting: Dalmatians in Film and Advertising". *Worldviews: Environment, Culture, Religion* **9**(2): 236–54.

Shell, M. 1986. "The Family Pet". *Representations* **15**: 121–53.

Shklovsky, V. 1988. "Art as Technique". In *Modern Criticism and Theory: A Reader*, D. Lodge (ed.), 16–30. Harlow: Longman.

Smith, J. A. 2003. "Beyond Dominance and Affection: Living with Rabbits in Post-Humanist Households". *Society & Animals* **11**(2): 181–97.

Smith, J. A. 2005. "'Viewing' the Body: Towards a Discourse of Animal Death". *Worldviews: Environment, Culture, Religion* **9**(2): 184–202.

Snow, N. E. 1991. "Compassion". *American Philosophical Quarterly* **28**(3): 195–205.

Spiegel, M. 1988. *The Dreaded Comparison*. London: Heretic Books.

Steeves, H. P. 2005. "Lost Dog, or, Levinas Faces the Animal". In *Figuring Animals: Essays on Animal Images in Art, Literature, Philosophy, and Popular Culture*, M. Sanders Pollock & C. Rainwater (eds), 21–35. Basingstoke: Palgrave.

Terhune, A. P. [1919] 1993. *Lad: A Dog*. Harmondsworth: Puffin.

Thomas, E. M. 2003. *The Hidden Life of Dogs*. London: Orion.

Tuan, Y.-F. 1984. *Dominance and Affection: The Making of Pets*. New Haven, CT: Yale University Press.

Tyler, A. 1995. *The Accidental Tourist*. London: Vintage.

Tyler, T. 2003. "If Horses Had Hands …". *Society & Animals* **11**(3), www.societyan-danimalsforum.org/sa/sa11.3/tyler.shtml (accessed July 2008).

Wasserman, E. 1993. "Eric Knight and *Lassie Come-Home*". In *Lassie: A Collie and Her Influence*, S, M. Brown (ed.), 18–23. St Louis, MO: The Dog Museum.

Wolfe, C. 2003. *Animal Rites: American Culture, the Discourse of Species, and Posthumanist Theory*. Chicago, IL: University of Chicago Press.

Woolf, V. 1998. *Flush*. Oxford: Oxford University Press.

Index